THE NEW LITERACY BLOCK

A simple, practical framework that is evidence-based, makes every minute count, and reaches all students

Lisa Donohue

Nicole Town

Pembroke Publishers Limited

© 2025 Pembroke Publishers
538 Hood Road
Markham, Ontario, Canada L3R 3K9
www.pembrokepublishers.com

All rights reserved.

No part of this publication may be reproduced in any form or by any means electronic or mechanical, including photocopy, scanning, recording, or any information, storage or retrieval system, without permission in writing from the publisher. Excerpts from this publication may be reproduced under licence from Access Copyright, or with the express written permission of Pembroke Publishers Limited, or as permitted by law.

Every effort has been made to contact copyright holders for permission to reproduce borrowed material. The publishers apologize for any such omissions and will be pleased to rectify them in subsequent reprints of the book.

Library and Archives Canada Cataloguing in Publication

Title: The new literacy block : a simple, practical framework that is evidence-based, makes every minute count, and reaches all students / Lisa Donohue, Nicole Town.

Names: Donohue, Lisa, author | Town, Nicole, author.

Description: Includes bibliographical references and index.

Identifiers: Canadiana (print) 20250246651 | Canadiana (ebook) 20250246716 | ISBN 9781551383767 (softcover) | ISBN 9781551389752 (PDF)

Subjects: LCSH: Literacy—Study and teaching (Elementary)

Classification: LCC LB1576 .D66 2025 | DDC 372.6/044—dc23

Editor: Kat Mototsune, Peter Buck
Cover Design: John Zehethofer
Typesetting: Jay Tee Graphics Ltd.

Printed and bound in Canada
9 8 7 6 5 4 3 2 1

Contents

Introduction *5*
Acknowledgments *7*

Chapter 1: 100 Minutes to Manage Literacy *9*

Making Every Minute Count *11*
    The Science: What Does *Structured Literacy* Mean? *11*
    A Comprehensive Approach to a Literacy Framework *13*

Chapter 2: The Building Blocks *16*

A Framework for Instruction *16*
    Why Direct Instruction Is Important *17*
    Building Stamina *18*
    Incorporating Choice *21*
    Building in Small-Group Instruction *22*
    Constructing Purposeful Practice Time *24*
    Tracking Purposeful Practice Time *27*
    Building in Accountability *29*
Building Blocks in Place *32*

Chapter 3: Composition: Writing, Speaking, Creating *38*

The Composition Process *39*
    Direct Instruction in Composition: Writing *41*
Exploring Purpose and Audience *44*
    Using Writing Prompts *45*
    Common Ground for Composition Purposes *53*

Chapter 4: Purposeful Practice of Composition *67*

From Composition Time to Independent Composing *68*
    Composition Cycle *69*
    Why This Instructional Sequence Is So Powerful *70*
Constructing Purposeful Practice Time *70*
    Building Stamina—Composition Routine *71*
Embedding Foundational Language Skills *76*
    Transition Activities and Words Skills Cycle *77*

Chapter 5: Comprehension: Reading, Listening, Viewing *83*

Reading Comprehension as an Outcome *84*
    The Neuroscience of Learning to Read *85*
Comprehension and the Literacy Block *86*
    Read-Alouds *88*
    What Is Text? *92*
    Talking About Texts *93*

Chapter 6: Purposeful Practice of Comprehension *99*

From Comprehension Time to Independent Reading *100*
   Comprehension Cycle *101*
Constructing Purposeful Practice Time *102*
   Building Stamina—Comprehension Routine *103*
   Responding to Texts—Comprehension Routine *107*
Embedding Digital Literacy and Cross-curricular Learning *112*
   Tech Time Cycle *112*
Putting It All Together *113*

Chapter 7: Flexible Small-Group Instruction *121*

Forming Instructional Groups *122*
   Purposeful Practice Groupings *123*
   Small-Group Instructional Clusters *123*
Small-Group Instruction and Intervention *124*

Chapter 8: Feedback and Assessment *126*

Beginning with the End in Mind *126*
   Learning Goals and Success Criteria *127*
Developing Assessment *For*, *As*, and *Of* Writing *128*
   Mentor Texts *128*
   Exemplars *129*
Feedback, Feedback, Feedback *133*
   Engaging in Assessment *As* Learning *135*
   Tracking Student Goals *136*

Chapter 9: Building Literacy Connections and Applications *139*

Authentically Developing Literacy Skills *140*
   Transferable Skills *141*
   Digital and Media Literacy Skills *143*
   Applications, Connections, and Contributions *145*

A Final Word *148*

Professional Resources *151*
Index *155*

Introduction

This book is a labour of love that we didn't anticipate writing. Throughout our careers, we have seen plenty of books about isolated elements of literacy that examined the pieces of the literacy block in a detailed and thorough manner. However, as we have worked with our colleagues in various capacities, the same challenges seem to surface. The question that gets asked the most frequently is this: "How do you fit it all in?"

When we begin to examine literacy, it is easy to be overwhelmed by the number of skills, strategies, and elements that fit under the umbrella of the term. In a regular instructional day, a typical literacy block contains approximately 100 minutes. But what exactly needs to fit into that time? When we think of all the elements of literacy learning, a list starts to form: phonemic awareness, decoding, word reading and spelling, morphology, vocabulary, fluency, language conventions, cursive writing, oral and non-verbal communications, critical thinking and comprehension strategies, text genres, forms and patterns, and digital media literacy skills to engage with various technologies. But this is just a start.

Structured Literacy is "a science-based approach to literacy instruction that is explicit, systematic and cumulative" (International Dyslexia Association, n.d., para. 7). However, in order to support the development of literate students, we have to include much more than the simple view of reading or the strands of Scarborough's Reading Rope. Comprehensive literacy instruction asks us to

- provide opportunities for students to think, talk, and share
- conference with small groups of students and individuals
- plan time for students to examine exemplars and model texts in order to create success criteria
- have students provide and receive feedback with their peers and teacher
- build in rich tasks, higher-order thinking, open-ended questions, and collaborative learning opportunities
- integrate digital literacy skills and technology by teaching students to analyze and create media works and to think critically and analytically about the texts they encounter online
- provide opportunities for students to have choice and voice in their learning, to capitalize on their own strengths, to identify areas for growth and set personal learning goals
- differentiate instruction to ensure that all students are demonstrating their learning in ways that are meaningful and relevant to them
- integrate learning from other subject areas and find texts that students can connect to

- teach students to write in a variety of text forms, including fiction and non-fiction, to write for a variety of purposes and audiences, and to read and think critically
- encourage students to write with voice and passion
- use ongoing assessment to monitor and evaluate students' learning and to guide our instruction
- accommodate students with different learning styles and modify instruction for students with differing abilities
- foster a love for learning

It's no wonder that the challenge of structuring a literacy block seems completely overwhelming—not to mention having to fit it into a limited amount of literacy time.

Although literacy blocks can differ in length, it is possible to fit all of these important aspects into a weekly cycle of instruction. By chunking a literacy block into distinct sections, it *is* possible to provide students opportunities to engage in all aspects of literacy every week. With this model, it *is* possible to provide daily explicit and systematic instruction in both comprehension and composition, and to meet regularly with every student for small-group instruction and intervention. It *is* possible to integrate technology, promote higher-order thinking, and engage students in their learning through tasks that provide opportunities for voice, choice, and agency. It *is* possible to form meaningful connections between the work that students are doing independently and the learning that is happening in other areas of literacy instruction. It *is* possible to build assessment right into the literacy block so that students receive immediate purposeful feedback. It *is* possible to do all of this and keep your sanity … we promise!

Acknowledgments

> **Land Acknowledgment**
>
> This book is written on land located on the traditional lands of the Wendat, Haudenosaunee, and the Anishinaabe peoples and the treaty land of the Williams Treaties First Nations and other Indigenous peoples whose presence here continues to this day. We thank them for sharing this land with us.
>
> So much of what we have been privileged to learn comes as a result of the land we live and work on, along with honouring the relationships with neighbors such as the Chippewas of Georgina Island First Nation and other Urban Indigenous people. We acknowledge our commitment to the continuous work of building a cooperative and respectful relationship through our learning and relearning of the process of reconciliation.

This book is a blend of new theory, existing classroom pedagogy, evidence-based and ongoing research, valuable sources, and trusted resources. Many people have influenced and supported me along the way, and I appreciate each and every one of them.

To my partners at Pembroke, Mary Macchiusi, Kat Mototsune, and Peter Buck: Thank you for your belief in my ability to bring new life to *100 Minutes*. Your organization and attention to detail have brought this book back and kept me on track to deliver a much-needed resource for educators.

Thanks to Jana Girdaskis (member of Mohawks of the Bay of Quinte) for taking the time to help me work things through and providing me with invaluable guidance and advice. You have played a vital role in helping me intentionally weave the principles and pedagogy of Storywork in key places throughout the book. Thank you for being such a conscientious leader, for helping me frame my thinking, for assisting me to remain appreciative in my approach to Indigenous education, and for being a true friend.

To my colleagues and fellow teachers: You have challenged me, been supportive thought-partners, enriched my classroom practice, and helped me to learn, unlearn, and refine my pedagogical approach to education. I am lucky to have had many collaborative opportunities with educational leaders who have made great contributions to my learning. To the colleagues turned friends: Thank you for providing endless support, feedback, and the validation I needed as I considered what this book could become.

At the beginning of my career, I was blessed with a gifted mentor. Her guidance, support, friendship, and cheerleading(!) have been a staple throughout my career and continue to shape the teacher and leader that I am today. Thank you, Lisa, for trusting me with your baby; I hope I made you proud.

Growing up a Town has been another great privilege in my life. Mom and Dad, your love and unwavering confidence in my potential are a big part of why this came together. Now there's more than one author in the family!

Finally, much of my learning and inspiration comes from my greatest loves, my husband and our children. Thank you for continually putting up with my mess on the dining room table, the endless teacher resources being delivered for me to read, and my general distractedness as I worked to complete this book. Quinn and Brooke, you've taught me more than anyone, and I am proud to be your mom—you are my greatest joy. Reid, thank you for your acceptance and patience as I let my passion for literacy and education take over these past few months. You are my sounding board when I need to rant, my confidant that I trust more than anyone to have my best interests at heart, my partner in all things, my better half, and my best friend. I love you more.

1   100 Minutes to Manage Literacy

A lot has changed since we began teaching together over 15 years ago. Lisa was my (Nikki's) mentor and I had so much to learn. I remember setting up my first classroom. The school year had already begun and I was hired on contract since a school that opened that September was understaffed. I was so keen to have everything look great, and then Lisa asked me, "But what are you going to teach tomorrow?"

Gone were the three-page lesson plans I had written in teacher's college. It was time to think bigger. I was no longer teaching one or two consecutive lessons. I needed to think about how to manage my instructional time. Literacy, I'll admit, seemed the most daunting: 100 minutes a day. That is a total of 500 minutes, or 8 hours and 20 minutes, of weekly language instruction. It is an immense chunk of time!

We would sit and plan (grade partner and mentor) to determine what needed to be done. We knew that students needed to read, write, spell, and learn grammar. Those were the basics, the fundamentals we knew about at the time. I worked to fill hour after hour, day after day, with guided reading activities and worksheets and guided and independent writing, and eventually even added guided inquiry to our practice. I was balancing literacy and gradually releasing the responsibility of learning to my students through a series of learning lessons and tasks. We discussed considerations such as the context of a lesson (where it fits in the teaching/learning cycle) and curriculum expectations. I needed to plan and implement assessment for learning to check the students' understanding and be responsive to each individual's needs. The line that regularly formed at the horseshoe table was overwhelming when students were working independently but had questions and wanted support with tasks.

As we worked together to plan for instruction, I knew that the writing process had multiple steps (pre-writing, drafting, writing, editing, and publishing), although I was unsure how to help each child at each stage. How could I possibly conference with each student as they were editing their rough copies? As students went through the whole writing process, they spent hours rewriting second drafts and final copies of their work. It left little time for writing just for the joy of it. Supporting writers to grow a love for writing and creating and sharing seemed out of reach and beyond the time we had available.

As for reading, we read together. We modelled and shared reading by reading stories as a class, with each child taking a turn to read out loud. Simple questions were asked to assess comprehension and students answered them. Comprehension needed to be assessed and monitored. But what did that mean? Was writing about their reading the best way to monitor it? The beginnings of understanding the importance of diagnostic assessment were there. Once that assessment was done, however, what did we do with the data? In a feeble attempt at differentiation, students were divided into groups based on their level and worked within those groups for months at a time to build their skills.

Day after day, the literacy block became 100 minutes filled with reading and writing work with some oral language and media literacy sprinkled in. Gradually, the busy routines of a language program seemed to fill the time. In fact, we were so successful at filling the 100-minute literacy block that it sometimes became difficult to find time to let students read independently or to read aloud to them. Dropping everything to read was important, but finding the time to read for pleasure somehow seemed wasteful of the limited available instructional minutes.

Time passed. Years went by. In settling into the busy routine of filling our days with guided reading and writing conferences, new challenges arose to commandeer our time. We worked hard, doing the best we could, but for some reason it wasn't working for every child. Fixing that became the challenge.

Although we were implementing guided reading and working with small groups of students on texts specifically chosen for their ability and interest, they were still not catching up to age/grade levels of reading. What if these students needed help with something we didn't know? The focus had always been on reading to learn, but some of these students were struggling to read, let alone learn from the text in front of them. There was no way that I would be able to work every day with an even greater number of small groups while the rest of the students were in the classroom. What on earth would the rest of the kids do while I sat with this one group of kids? The classroom would certainly erupt in total anarchy. Still, the Science of Reading was gaining traction, and it felt like this was the direction we needed to follow. And then a new curriculum was dropped!

So, with the support of many colleagues, we began to experiment with the concept of small-group instruction based on the strengths and needs of our students rather than the level of their reading ability. By color-coding data, we began to see patterns in the strengths and the areas of need in our classrooms. But was the data we were collecting telling us the whole story? We continued to wonder how to help students make intentional connections between the things we were learning together and the things they were practicing independently. We needed to target our instruction and be culturally relevant and responsive in our practice in order to build an inclusive school/classroom culture.

As we examined our practice and pedagogy, we questioned the authenticity of tasks. Where was the choice we were supposed to be providing? The list of considerations and things we needed to attend to for our students continued to grow and grow. We needed to target student engagement, foster autonomy, promote higher-order thinking, build in opportunities for accountable talk, make meaningful connections to other content areas and to the world around us, while also working to help raise global citizens who see the world as an interconnected place and understand that their classrooms may have walls but not boundaries. At the same time, we needed to continue to help students connect, collaborate, create, and communicate, both face-to-face and through the use of digital tools. We needed to use rather than teach technology, and simultaneously build on the solid foundations of reading, writing, listening, speaking, viewing, and creating. Moreover, we needed to teach students to evaluate, integrate, and consolidate. The only thing that remained the same was that we still needed to accomplish this in 100 minutes of the day, 500 minutes a week, for a total of 8 hours and 20 minutes of literacy instruction every week. Now the time hardly seemed adequate. Was it even possible to structure a literacy block to address all the required components of literacy? How could we reasonably target such a vast array of learning?

Making Every Minute Count

The publication of *100 Minutes: Making Every Minute Count in the Literacy Block* affirmed a model for a 100-minute literacy block that supported the work happening in my classroom. The model was based on the fundamental belief that students need time for explicit teaching, time for purposeful practice, and time for independent work. Students need to have choice in their learning and to have their individual voices heard. Technology should never be an additional thing to teach; it should instead be an integrated component of daily instruction. Higher-order thinking can be fostered through the vehicle of accountable talk. And above all, students should always see their learning as important, relevant, and authentic.

Although the demands of literacy instruction seem far more complex today than when I first started teaching, the essential underlying principles listed above are still very relevant. The use of a consistent framework can make it possible for all students to engage in the essential components of literacy, to make meaningful connections between the things they are learning through instruction and independent practice, and to have frequent opportunities for feedback, goal-setting, and ongoing assessment. With the growing demands of literacy instruction, it is more important than ever to ensure we have the building blocks to construct a solid foundation for our students to become critically literate individuals.

As teachers, we want a framework for learning that maximizes every minute we spend with our students; a structure that provides simple strategies for differentiation and includes choice and agency; a structure that seamlessly integrates digital literacy, cross-curricular learning, critical thinking and problem-solving, communication, self-directed learning, and time for collaboration; a structure that provides teachers with the opportunity to meet the needs of all students; a structure that does it all in 100 minutes (or less!).

The Science: What Does *Structured Literacy* Mean?

> "Structured Literacy is characterized by the provision of systematic, explicit instruction that integrates listening, speaking, reading, and writing and emphasizes the structure of language across the speech sound system (phonology), the writing system (orthography), the structure of sentences (syntax), the meaningful parts of words (morphology), the relationships among words (semantics), and the organization of spoken and written discourse." (International Dyslexia Association, 2019)

As we begin to think of the best ways to utilize the daily literacy block, we need an understanding of what *Structured Literacy* means, especially as it relates to the *Science of Reading*. According to the International Dyslexia Association (2019), Structured Literacy is an approach to instruction where teachers intentionally structure important literacy skills, concepts, and the sequence of instruction to meet the developmental needs of students as much as possible, while they carefully guide the students' literacy learning and progress. This is a shift from a balanced literacy approach as we move from guided reading instruction to whole-class and small-group instruction that is both systematic and explicit.

Does that mean we disregard all the work that came before? Does that mean that, as we learn more about the Science of Reading and evidence-based practices, we declare our current literacy practices no longer relevant? I don't think so. I believe that, as educators, we are always working toward *better* practices, evolving along with our profession, and it is vital that we be kind to ourselves as we shift our instruction and assessment to better align with what the neuroscience is telling us. To clarify, the Science of Reading is the neuroscience, a body of research that informs our practice and provides us with the knowledge we need to understand how children learn to read. This science then informs our instructional practices (Structured Literacy) so they are adequately evidence-based to support student achievement. We can then see Multi-Tiered Systems of Support (MTSS) as the delivery model for the evidence-based instruction of Structured Literacy. As educators, we need to take a tiered approach if we are not only to include the fundamentals of reading, writing, listening, and speaking, but also build upon students' skills in a systematic progression with engaging, multimodal activities. At the same time, we need to vary the vehicles through which we learn and communicate (print and online texts, digital tools, media texts, collaborative learning, critical thinking and problem-solving). According to the Center on Multi-Tiered System of Supports at the American Institutes for Research (2025), the essential components of MTSS include screening (assessment), progress monitoring, data-based decision-making, and a multi-level prevention system. In this evidence-based framework, students are supported with instruction and intervention that increases and intensifies across three tiers of instructional approaches. The flexible structure of the three tiers allows students to receive instruction and intensive supports based on their needs as determined through the collection of targeted assessment data.

A comprehensive literacy program with MTSS means much more than just providing opportunities for students to participate in reading and writing in a single day. There are several important components of Structured Literacy that support all students in developing essential literacy knowledge and skills. Across all disciplines, subjects, and divisions, our role as literacy educators is to create the spaces and learning circumstances where students can explore the joy, hope, and pathways that literacy learning can ignite (Ontario Ministry of Education, 2023, Language curriculum Vision and Goals section). Therefore, there is no one program or method, but rather approaches that align with the principles of Structured Literacy *and* best meet the needs of the specific students in a particular community given the available resources.

All students need routines to be successful. But without constant revisiting, routines become mundane, boring, and monotonous. I'm not saying that we should abandon routines; nothing could be further from the truth. The only way to build stamina and independence is with consistent routines. However, these routines need to continue to deepen, be responsive, and become richer as the year progresses. Students need to add layers to their routines, adding choices and agency to enhance their learning experiences.

As we work through the different components of a literacy block, we will begin to see these layers emerge with all the things our students need. We structure their experiences not only from one day to the next, but also from week to week and ultimately from month to month through the year. The growing sophistication, or deepening, of the tasks allows students to continue their learning, broaden their thinking, and inspire curiosity. By establishing strong consistent routines and then not only maintaining them but enriching them, we are able to create a truly dynamic literacy time in which all students are able to engage in a wide variety of rich learning tasks.

If we were to try to teach each of the elements of Structured Literacy in isolation, we would certainly need more than 100 minutes a day. In fact, there are probably not enough hours in the school day to address all these areas independently. However, through the use of intentionally crafted blocks of time, we can build literacy routines that create the foundation for a flexible structure that can be adapted to be responsive to the students in front of us and better utilize MTSS.

If teaching were like cooking, we'd be able to consistently follow a recipe, or a prescribed set of steps, and successfully teach every student, every year. It would be comforting to know that completing a given checklist of literary experiences would fulfill the requirement of teaching literacy in a structured way. However, there is no one recipe or list that meets the tastes of our ever-changing classrooms and communities. Although there are elements of literacy that must be included every day, once routines become stale and mundane, student engagement quickly decreases. The challenge we face as educators is to find a way of enriching routines and adding to them over time in such a way that students are able to select from a wide variety of activities within familiar routines.

When we build a literacy block, we need to begin with a solid foundation. That foundation is based on the simple routines of the core elements of the block. These elements remain essentially the same throughout the year, but they continue to be the framework that holds all the other pieces in place. As the year progresses, we need to add new layers to our block, with each layer bringing a new level of complexity and sophistication. As we add to our students' literary experiences, we need to ensure that we are fostering independence at each level. Each new experience brings with it a new set of learning goals and expectations. We need to make sure that, as we introduce our students to these new layers, we take the time to ensure that they are confident with not only the routines, but also the learning goals each new experience brings. Taking the time to introduce students to all tasks, share learning goals, model sample work, and co-construct success criteria will ensure that everyone shares a common understanding of the expectations of all tasks.

Building a literacy block takes time. There is no way that students can begin a school year in the fall and immediately jump into rich, differentiated, independent, and shared learning experiences in all areas of literacy. That becomes our goal over time. As students begin to develop a comfort level with the expectations set for them, we know it is time to begin to add another layer to our instruction. There is a fine balance between fostering routines and creating monotony. Bored students are often disengaged students, and their level of performance is reduced. Doing the same thing day after day, week after week, month after month is a formula that would certainly result in student fatigue and lack of interest. If we add new dimensions to these familiar routines, we encourage students to see them in fresh new ways. The routines can then serve as a comfortable framework on which they are able to build new learning experiences.

A Comprehensive Approach to a Literacy Framework

The key to forming a framework for a literacy block that can effectively meet all the requirements of a comprehensive literacy program is to divide the block into smaller blocks of time. Within these blocks of time, a tiered approach to instruction and assessment is manageable, providing the necessary support and accommodations that enable teachers to remove barriers and allow students to thrive. The continuum of support provided through MTSS helps teachers build a fluid and flexible framework that can be responsive to student needs and driven by student data. Teachers can provide daily whole-class instruction in both comprehension and composition, as well as daily small-group instruction. Students are able to engage in a wide range of independent and collaborative activities directly connected to their learning. Teachers are able to monitor progress and provide immediate feedback on students' work, helping them to set realistic goals that will continue to drive their learning forward. By creating flexible chunks of time within the literacy block, we are able to teach in ways that are responsive to our students' needs but remain firmly grounded in the learning goals and expectations.

The literacy framework outlined in this book comprises three distinct blocks of time. Two of these provide time for direct instruction in comprehension and composition; the third allows time for students to work independently or in small groups. As students work independently, they are applying their writing and reading daily and engaging in Purposeful Practice. During direct-instruction Comprehension and Composition Time, teachers can explicitly teach students about the various skills associated with comprehension (reading, listening, and viewing), and composition (writing, speaking, and creating). During Purposeful Practice Time, students can apply this learning to their own work. This time presents the teacher with valuable opportunities to work with small groups of students for additional instruction as well as for targeted intensive support in reading and writing.

This framework also provides embedded opportunities for students to learn, practice, and apply new skills through the gradual release of responsibility. In this framework, the teacher introduces the students to new learning through modelling and direct instruction. Then, through small-group instruction, the teacher is able to support, monitor, and provide feedback to students as they begin to apply and integrate their new learning. Finally, students are able to work on their own in order to use this new learning independently. As most teachers know, it is necessary to engage students and support their learning in a variety of ways, such as using direct instruction to systematically and explicitly teach foundational knowledge and skills, and providing numerous opportunities for guided practice, descriptive feedback, modelling, and coaching. In order for students to acquire new literacy skills and strengthen existing ones, the teacher needs to begin by explicitly modelling and giving direct instruction on effective strategies; then using small-group instruction as a vehicle for coaching, guiding, and providing feedback; supporting students as they begin to practice new skills; and finally building in opportunities for students to work independently to apply their new learning.

By including two chunks of time for whole-group instruction and time for students to engage in independent shared and guided learning experiences, the 100-minute framework provides opportunities for the gradual release of responsibility to be seamlessly integrated into all literacy experiences. As students transition from large-group to small-group instruction and then to independent work, they are introduced to new skills, guided through them, and finally encouraged to practice and apply them.

THE BASICS

Each chunk of time in a literacy block can be used for a variety of purposes, and the instructional content will broaden and change as the year progresses. However, for simplicity's sake, we'll start with the basics.

Transition Activities: This is a brief chunk of time—10 minutes maximum—at the beginning of the literacy block when students engage in ongoing short, sharp, and shiny word work exercises. These warm-up activities can involve phonics, word patterns, syllabication of words, morphology, and more, helping students develop into better readers and writers by providing focused time for understanding and manipulating words. It can also allow time for students to get settled and engaged in the classroom learning environment.

Composition Time: Imagine the first chunk of time as a 20- to 30-minute whole-class lesson. The teacher could use this time to model writing for various purposes; introduce new forms of writing; create success criteria with students; have students engage in collaborative composition activities; explicitly teach writing skills, such as descriptive writing, writing with voice, writing for an audience, vocabulary usage, and figurative language; teach grammar and sentence fluency; and much more.

Purposeful Practice Time: The second chunk is a slightly longer period of time—approximately 40 minutes—when students have the opportunity to work independently, collaboratively, or in small groups on a wide range of tasks. These could include independent reading, responding to texts, independent writing, word skills, accessing technology, building digital literacy skills through media study, and opportunities for sharing with peers and for giving and receiving feedback. While students are working on these tasks, the teacher would have the opportunity to meet with various groups of students. This time spent in small groups could be for a purposeful focus such as decoding instruction, building morphology or vocabulary skills, fluency practice, writing conferences, or any other lesson for which students might need small-group direct instruction. This time can also be flexible by being split up into cycles, with one following Composition Time and the other following Comprehension Time.

Comprehension Time: The third and final chunk of time—another block of 20 to 30 minutes—could be used for whole-class instruction again, with a focus on language comprehension. Using the Science of Reading to inform our practice, this time could be used for direct instruction in decoding (reading) or focused on modelling fluency through reading aloud to students, modelling thinking aloud and explicitly introducing various thinking moves, posing critical-thinking questions, and encouraging students to talk with each other about various texts. This instructional time could also be an opportunity to engage with a wider variety of texts, such as oral stories, podcasts, visual media such as infographics, or short film texts. During this time, the teacher might also choose to introduce different reading responses, model sample responses, and set learning goals with students related to their reading and engagement with a variety of texts.

You will notice that the durations of the elements are varied and flexible. Within this suggested framework, flexibility is paramount. As all learners are different, so are all classes. A longer instructional time may work for one group of learners, while it might need to be shortened for another. Some learners thrive during the independent work time; others might need to move quickly from one activity to another to remain engaged. As with all instructional frameworks, teachers should consider these strategies suggestions rather than hard and fast rules. Teachers should adjust their literacy routines in ways that best meet the needs of their students as they get to know them. A teacher should be part artist, part scientist, part psychologist, and part gymnast—flexibility is always the greatest gift we can give ourselves and our students. I remember my mother—a teacher herself—quoting an old proverb: "Blessed are the flexible, for they shall not be bent out of shape."

2 The Building Blocks

At the beginning of a new year, it is important to set the tone that will carry through the remainder of the year. By taking the time to establish strong, structured literacy routines, you can ensure that students are engaged in meaningful learning in all aspects of literacy. Students need to have a clear understanding of the various elements of the daily/weekly literacy routine.

A Framework for Instruction

The first element to introduce into a literacy block should be the times dedicated to whole-class direct instruction. In one model I will propose, these times bookend the literacy block, comprising the beginning and the end of the 100 minutes. In another model, these times break up the Purposeful Practice Time to allow the educator to build students' stamina toward independent work time that is flexible and provides opportunities for choice and agency. Neither of these models need to be adhered to for the entire school year. Educators must remain flexible and responsive to their students' needs and adapt their literacy planning and instruction as necessary.

As we introduce the building blocks, it is also important to consider how our schools and classrooms are working with students and families to celebrate who students are. Using Culturally Relevant and Responsive Pedagogy (CRRP) to build learning communities is vital in supporting students' academic, social, emotional, and physical well-being and success.

> CRRP is a research-based pedagogy that has been around for many years and has proven to positively impact family engagement and student achievement. It is not a framework that can be quickly implemented, nor is it a set of lesson plans or activities. It is a shift in how we think about ourselves, students, families and communities and how we use lived experiences and culture to ensure equitable outcomes for all students. (McAuley, S., 2018)

Most teachers have a selection of community-building activities they choose to introduce at the beginning of the year, from icebreakers and inclusion activities/games to determination of a class set of agreements. These activities are highly valuable in fostering a sense of belonging and connection, establishing a positive climate and a sense of community for students, as well as promoting transferable skills such as collaboration and communication. Using the literacy block for some of these activities is an option.

It is possible even in the first week of school to introduce students to these first two elements of the literacy block. By carving out some time in the literacy block, you can begin to set up the routines that will be foundational for the entire year. You might start a literacy block with Composition Time consisting of whole-class writing instruction or word work that sets the tone for a positive, focused learning environment. For example, in the beginning days of school you might explicitly teach a few lessons on orthographic mapping to introduce students to the morphological word work activities that will build your transition time. Or perhaps you'll model a composition task, such as writing a letter to the students, creating an infographic of class facts or a class contract of agreements, or even generating discussion that reflects on students' hopes for the coming year.

Likewise, you will want to add Comprehension Time consisting of a whole-class reading lesson, such as reading a picture book aloud to students. Posing a few thoughtful questions to students can gain you some insight into the group of learners as a whole. In the first few days of school, this will be a time you can use to read aloud to students and begin to actively teach them how to engage in conversations with each other. Whatever the content, the students will be introduced to the way the time will be used for focused direct instruction.

As time goes on, these two blocks will form the foundation for all whole-class literacy instruction. They will introduce students to purposes for composition and forms of writing and model fluent reading and the comprehension strategies we use to understand increasingly complex texts. Students will learn to apply critical thinking skills and brainstorm potential topics for composition and writing that foster their global citizenship and sustainability mentality. The two blocks will form the foundational component of direct instruction in which you actively teach the big ideas of the literacy curriculum and make transferable skills, such as collaboration, communication, and digital literacy, visible for students.

Why Direct Instruction Is Important

In whole-class learning experiences, the teacher explicitly teaches effective literacy strategies. As already mentioned, explicit and systematic instruction are important elements of Structured Literacy. The Ontario Language Curriculum defines explicit instruction as "provid[ing] clear, direct, purposeful teaching of specific knowledge, skills, and strategies" (Ontario Ministry of Education, 2023, Instructional Approaches in Language section, para. 7), while at the same time outlining that "systematic instruction involves a carefully planned sequence for instruction of specific concepts, skills, and procedures, with the prerequisite skills taught first" (Ontario Ministry of Education, 2023, Instructional Approaches in Language section, para. 8).

Therefore, direct instruction provides teachers with the opportunity to systematically introduce concepts and explicitly teach literacy content and strategies. It is a time when the teacher can model fluency and demonstrate thinking aloud so students become aware of what happens in a reader's head when that person is reading and thinking about texts. It is a time for introducing new text forms and for reinforcing students' understanding of purposes for composition and the considerations of various audiences for writing. It is a time for mini-lessons in grammar and word skills, ensuring that these remain grounded in authentic reading and writing experiences. It is a time for students to explore higher-order thinking questions by engaging in discussions about texts. It is a time when teachers can pose open-ended questions and encourage students to think, question, share, explore, and justify their ideas. It is a time when teachers can monitor understanding and provide timely feedback to the group of learners as a whole.

You might find this chart helpful when building the literacy block. When you take the time to establish the various literacy elements in a logical sequential way, students can use the allotted time to maximize their learning—in a whole-class group, in a small-group setting, or working independently. In the first week or two of school, organizing your literacy block in the following way will provide a foundation for future elements.

THE LITERACY BLOCK: INTRODUCING DIRECT INSTRUCTION

Approximate time	Literacy Activity	
15–30 minutes	**Direct Instruction: Composition and Word Skills**	
	Teacher	Students
	Composition and/or Word Skills Teaching students various composition or word skills competencies through explicit instruction, modelling, examination of mentor texts, establishing success criteria, etc.	**Whole Class** Active participation in lesson and various activities to build foundational knowledge.
Flexible	Teacher-selected community-building activities	
15–30 minutes	**Direct Instruction: Comprehension and Fluency**	
	Teacher	Students
	Comprehension and/or Fluency Teaching students how to engage with texts by reading aloud, explicitly teaching decoding and fluency strategies, posing critical thinking questions, exploring diverse world views and perspectives, etc.	**Whole Class** Active participation in lesson and various activities to build background knowledge.

Note: In all following charts of the Literacy Block, repeated elements are shaded.

Building Stamina

As early as the first or second week of school, teachers can begin to introduce students to independent learning routines. These routines will require stamina-building and will take days, if not weeks, to establish successfully. They will also need to be revisited and reestablished after periods of change, such as a school break or when new students are added to the class. Patience and consistency are the keys to developing these essential elements. During independent work time, students will practice, transfer, and apply the learning that takes place in all other areas of the literacy block. You need to establish clear, consistent expectations for these times to enable all students to focus on their own learning.

The time invested in the first weeks of school to set the stage for focused independent learning will be greatly valued as the year progresses. Independent work times make all small-group instruction possible. It is essential that these routines be firmly established in the first weeks of school. Here are some examples of routines you may wish to establish to support the management of time and behavior in the classroom:

- *Waiting Room:* Write the numbers 1 to 9 on clothespins and attach them to a basket or poster on a bulletin board labelled "Waiting Room." Just like at the deli counter at a supermarket, students take a number if they have a question instead of interrupting the teacher while they're working with a small group. This gives the student confidence that they will get time with the teacher while allowing them to move onto something else so they can come back to their question when the teacher is available. The teacher can take a break between groups and call, "Now serving number 3!"
- *Visual Timer:* Set up a timer that students can see. This often supports students in managing their time as they see what amount of time is left for them to focus on a task before they switch their attention to the next activity. The timer can be as simple as a countdown video, or you could use a kitchen timer with a noise that cues students to change activities.
- *Visual Schedule:* Create a task board where you lay out the activities that students will be working on for the duration of their Purposeful Practice Time. Later in this chapter, examples and reproducibles that can support the use of this strategy will be provided.
- *Questions Board:* On a board, write common questions students have about completing a task, along with their answers, so they can refer back to your instructions without interrupting small-group instruction. For example: *Who can I work with? Where can I work? What materials do I need? Where do I hand it in?* In the past, I have actually made magnets with visuals of these so I can just put them up without writing them each time.
- *Ask 3 Before Me:* This simple routine can help students find support from their peers before they interrupt small-group instructional time to speak with the teacher. I would also ask students to start with their group members in an effort to stop them wandering around the classroom.
- *Resource Station:* Set up a station within the class where students have access to commonly used classroom materials so they are not asking the teacher (or interrupting a friend!) when they need something like a pencil, an eraser, or a ruler. If students are having trouble managing materials and you are running out of things quickly, you could also create special labels to ensure materials are returned at the end of class; for example, tape fake flowers onto the end of pencils for a fun look.

It is important to note that independent work is a learning skill that is assessed throughout the year and evaluated on the students' report card. This means the teacher is responsible for providing instruction and clear expectations or success criteria of reasonable demonstration of the learning skill. Providing time to discuss and set these expectations is vital, and there will be times throughout the year when the expectations set at the beginning of the year are revisited in order to ensure that students continue to use their independent work times in a way that maximizes their learning and the learning of others.

> "Reading volume is considered a fundamental principle of the science of reading, encompassing a wide array of research on effective literacy learning strategies. Research consistently indicates that the quantity of reading material consumed plays a pivotal role in reading development (Seidenberg, 2017). Even novice readers who engage extensively in reading demonstrate notable advancements in literacy and language skills compared with their less engaged counterparts (Hiebert, 2024)."
> (Bus, A. G., Shang, Y., & Roskos, K., 2024)

It is also critical to distinguish between independent work time and the practice of independent reading. Independent, self-selected reading time can be a significant indicator of student success. That being said, the practice of independent reading should not replace a comprehensive reading program in classrooms. (We will explore this in more detail in Chapter 5: *Comprehension: Reading, Viewing, Listening*.)

Within the first few weeks of school, the literacy block should be starting to take shape, including four basic elements that combine direct instruction and independent practice in both comprehension and composition. This chart may be helpful when organizing a literacy block containing these four elements.

THE LITERACY BLOCK: INTRODUCING INDEPENDENT LEARNING

Approximate time	Literacy Activity	
15–30 minutes	**Direct Instruction: Composition and Word Skills**	
	Teacher	Students
	Composition and/or Word Skills Teaching students various composition or word skills competencies through explicit instruction, modelling, examination of mentor texts, establishing success criteria, etc.	**Whole Class** Active participation in lesson and various activities to build foundational knowledge.
10–20 minutes	**Independent Work**	
	Teacher	Students
	Once initial routine is established, this time can be used for completing individual or small-group assessment tasks.	**Independent Work** Working on task assigned by teacher (composition and/or word skills).
15–30 minutes	**Direct Instruction: Comprehension and Fluency**	
	Teacher	Students
	Comprehension and/or Fluency Teaching students how to engage with texts by reading aloud, explicitly teaching decoding and fluency strategies, posing critical thinking questions, exploring diverse world views and perspectives, etc.	**Whole Class** Active participation in lesson and various activities to build background knowledge.

10–20 minutes	**Independent Work**	
	Teacher	Students
	Once initial routine is established, this time can be used for completing individual or small-group assessment tasks.	**Independent Work** Working on task assigned by teacher (comprehension, fluency and/or decoding skills).

Incorporating Choice

One aspect of enacting culturally responsive and relevant pedagogy involves incorporating choice into student learning. Research has shown that when this is done, student engagement and achievement increases. Amosa *et al.* (2008) concluded that tasks that allow students to demonstrate their learning in a variety of ways score higher in intellectual quality, quality learning, and overall quality teaching. They also found that tasks scaffolded with clear instruction and a framework for learning, followed by creative tasks that were personally relevant for students, also score significantly higher.

Universal Design for Learning (UDL) is a philosophical framework that represents a proactive approach to curriculum design and delivery that involves a variety of opportunities for choice. The framework's objective is to foster inclusive learning environments and ensure equitable access to educational opportunities for all students based on cognitive neuroscience research investigating how the human brain learns. By intentionally building in flexibility and choice regarding how learners access information, engage in the learning process, and demonstrate their understanding, UDL-informed planning can enhance learning outcomes for diverse student populations, remove barriers, and build on students' strengths from an asset-based lens (Novak & Rodriguez, 2023). This approach ensures that educators plan for instruction that effectively builds upon what a student can do within the context of a learning continuum.

According to CAST (2024), UDL "aims to change the design of the environment rather than to situate the problem as a perceived deficit within the learner. When environments are intentionally designed to reduce barriers, every learner can engage in rigorous, meaningful learning." The guidelines offered by CAST (2024) are organized into three categories for designing multiple means for students: engagement, representation, and action and expression.

Choice can be woven into a literacy block in many different ways through UDL-informed planning and instruction. When engagement is taken into account, students can be provided time to work on a literacy activity of their choice within the area of literacy (comprehension, composition, or foundations of language) they would like to work on. In terms of representation, students can determine their choice of materials from a variety of provided texts by a range of authors representing a diversity of perspectives and identities. Finally, when action and expression are considered, students might choose how to demonstrate their learning from a selection of forms they can use to best convey their message.

Opportunities for students to choose can be embedded in all learning opportunities, while the teacher oversees or facilitates the choices they are making; i.e., the teacher chooses *what* the student is learning, and the students choose *how* they are learning it and/or how they are *representing* their learning. This will be explored in greater depth in later chapters.

In this fashion, the teacher and students work together so that all learning goals are being met, while the teacher orchestrates a routine that ensures all students have access to all aspects of literacy. This ensures that students regularly participate in all learning opportunities, instead of self-selecting their favorite literacy activities while neglecting other less desirable tasks. When choice is embedded within each activity, students can select how they would like to learn the skills that the teacher and curriculum require them to learn.

Building in Small-Group Instruction

Once the independent routines have been established, students can be introduced to small-group instruction, the heart and soul of the literacy block. It is the time when you can collect assessment data, provide targeted direct instruction based on various assessments, monitor individual student learning, give immediate feedback, and assist students in setting personal learning goals.

Now you ask yourself: what am I doing in small-group instruction? Small-group instruction should be targeted content specific to the student's needs, have an intentional timeline, and include opportunities to monitor progress to ensure that the educator remains flexible and responsive to the needs of each student.

A good place to start is to complete initial assessments of individual students that will allow you to find common areas of need in your class. A vital part of reading assessment is listening to a student read. This is why setting up these routines is an important part of meeting students' needs. They provide the necessary setting to conduct initial assessments to inform your instruction. A screener is a tool that can provide educators with the quick snapshot they need for initial assessments to help them determine small groups for targeted instruction. (More on this in Chapter 5: *Comprehension: Reading, Viewing, Listening*.)

As mentioned earlier, the educator is intentionally not included in the Purposeful Practice Time activities, allowing them to be flexible and pull individuals or groupings of students to be responsive to the instructional needs of the class. To support your formation of instructional groupings, educators will want to consider the following:

1. What is the focus for instruction?
2. Who has this learning need and requires targeted intervention (according to assessment data)?
3. What resources do I have available (or need to find) to support this instructional focus?

Using the information gathered from these questions, educators can then make informed instructional decisions to build small groups for direct, targeted intervention.

Another use you may consider adding to small-group time is a check-in with groups as they work on any of the given tasks. This can provide educators with the opportunity to monitor specific students or meet with additional students who may not be captured in your initial intervention groupings. It is also important to note that in MTSS, Tier 1 includes interventions for supporting students to meet grade-level expectations and opportunities to provide enrichment or extension of the learning. Therefore, each student should be included in at least one small-group instructional setting, with some students/groupings being seen more frequently depending on the focus for instruction.

> "A screening measure is a quick and informal evidence-based test that provides information about possible reading difficulties. It identifies students who are at risk for or currently experiencing reading difficulties so they can receive more instruction or immediate intervention.... It is an early detection strategy for the benefit of students and teachers. Teachers better understand how to help their students, and students receive immediate and targeted support." (Ontario Human Rights Commission, 2024)

> ### Instructional Groupings
>
> Students can be grouped in different ways in order to facilitate their learning. These groupings could include mixed-ability groups, talk-partners, instructional-level groupings, groupings by interest or topic, or self-selected partners. Instructional groupings can change according to the learning goals, the needs of the students, or the task itself. Students need to work with a variety of partners and groups in order to strengthen their collaborative skills and learn from the ideas of others. As students are organized into various groupings throughout the literacy block, the teacher and students can make many decisions that affect the way students are grouped. Flexibility and variety are the keys to success with student groupings.

This chart might be helpful when pacing out the literacy block as these new elements are added.

THE LITERACY BLOCK: INTRODUCING SMALL-GROUP INSTRUCTION

Approximate time	Literacy Activity	
15–30 minutes	**Direct Instruction: Composition and Word Skills**	
	Teacher	Students
	Composition and/or Word Skills Teaching students various composition or word skills competencies through explicit instruction, modelling, examination of mentor texts, establishing success criteria, etc.	**Whole Class** Active participation in lesson and various activities to build foundational knowledge.
10–20 minutes	**Independent Work**	
	Teacher	Students
	Small-group Instruction Working with a small group of students based on focus for instruction (composition and/or word skills).	**Independent Work** Working on task assigned by teacher (composition and/or word skills).

The Building Blocks

15–30 minutes	**Direct Instruction: Comprehension and Fluency**	
	Teacher	Students
	Comprehension and/or Fluency Teaching students how to engage with texts by reading aloud, explicitly teaching decoding and fluency strategies, posing critical thinking questions, exploring diverse world views and perspectives, etc.	**Whole Class** Active participation in lesson and various activities to build background knowledge.
10–20 minutes	**Independent Work**	
	Teacher	Students
	Small Group Instruction Working with a small group of students based on focus for instruction (comprehension, fluency, and/or decoding skills).	**Independent Work** Working on task assigned by teacher (comprehension, fluency, and/or decoding skills).

As you can see, the foundations of the literacy block are starting to take shape! The various elements of literacy instruction—including whole-class direct instruction and independent Purposeful Practice Time for students—are built into our consistent blocks of time, and classroom management routines are embedded to support students' independence. By revisiting these routines and expectations and through frequent reinforcement of students who are working well independently, it will now be possible to have a literacy block where independent Purposeful Practice Time creates opportunities for direct instruction in various comprehension and composition skills.

Constructing Purposeful Practice Time

For more on what those expectations and tasks could look like, see Chapters 4 and 6.

At this point in the building of the literacy block, students have developed an understanding of the various expectations for different independent tasks.

It then becomes possible to cluster these independent times to provide a greater block in which students can work with the teacher and then transfer and apply their learning. In this way, students would have an opportunity to participate in a whole-class mini-lesson and then attend small-group instruction to practice their fluency further or make targeted gains in building their decoding skills, followed by time working independently. This gives them an opportunity to transfer and apply the skills they have just learned, either in a small group or in a whole-class mini-lesson. Similarly, some students could begin with independent work time and then have a chance to share their work with a teacher in conference or through a peer-sharing activity. This kind of intentionality in the sequencing of tasks sets the Purposeful Practice Time outlined here apart from other literacy frameworks.

Structuring a literacy block so that students can regularly meet with the teacher allows for timely instruction, feedback, and transfer of learning. Students can be organized into groups in order to easily support the transitioning from one task to the other. While some tasks, such as Partner Reading and Peer Sharing, would be completed while students are working collaboratively, the remainder of tasks would be completed independently.

It will take students a while to become familiar with the transition to a literacy block that contains all the components of a comprehensive literacy program, but rest assured that the time already invested in establishing independent routines will now pay off. You will need to give students a signal so they know when to stop one independent task and begin another. This may be as simple as saying, "Take a few minutes to finish up your first task and get ready to begin your next one." Or you might choose a sound or visual signal that cues students to move on to their next task. Whatever routine you establish, consistency will be key.

Now the foundations of differentiation are in place. Students will be working on different tasks at different times, and you will be able to tailor small-group instruction to suit individual needs. It is also important to note that educators and students will not necessarily remain in this purposeful practice cycle every day of the week. To maintain the routines, you will often need to pause the cycle to allow time for whole-class instructional time that permits intentional direct instruction as a part of the gradual release of responsibility.

The following charts may help when chunking independent work times in order to form Purposeful Practice Time. Note that this chart is arranged twice below to model the entire literacy block in three or four distinct blocks of time, depending on your preference.

THREE-BLOCK MODEL

THE LITERACY BLOCK: INTRODUCING PURPOSEFUL PRACTICE TIME

Approximate time	Literacy Activity	
15–30 minutes	**Direct Instruction: Composition and Word Skills**	
	Teacher	Students
	Composition and/or Word Skills Teaching students various composition or word skills competencies through explicit instruction, modelling, examination of mentor texts, establishing success criteria, etc.	**Whole Class** Active participation in lesson and various activities to build foundational knowledge.
30–40 minutes (divided into two 15–20 minute work times)	**Purposeful Practice Time (round 1)**	
	Teacher	Students
	Small-Group Instruction Working with a small group of students based on focus for instruction (composition and/or word skills).	**Purposeful Practice Time** **Group 1:** Independent Reading **Group 2:** Partner Reading **Group 3:** Peer Sharing **Group 4:** Independent Composing

	Purposeful Practice Time (round 2)	
	Teacher	Students
	Small-Group Instruction Working with a small group of students based on focus for instruction (comprehension, fluency, and/or decoding skills).	**Purposeful Practice Time** **Group 1:** Responding to Texts **Group 2:** Responding to Texts **Group 3:** Independent Composing **Group 4:** Peer Sharing
15–30 minutes	**Direct Instruction: Comprehension and Fluency**	
	Teacher	Students
	Comprehension and/or Fluency Teaching students how to engage with texts by reading aloud, explicitly teaching decoding and fluency strategies, posing critical thinking questions, exploring diverse world views and perspectives, etc.	**Whole Class** Active participation in lesson and various activities to build background knowledge.

FOUR-BLOCK MODEL

THE LITERACY BLOCK: INTRODUCING PURPOSEFUL PRACTICE TIME

Approximate time	Literacy Activity	
15–30 minutes	**Direct Instruction: Composition and Word Skills**	
	Teacher	Students
	Composition and/or Word Skills Teaching students various composition or word skills competencies through explicit instruction, modelling, examination of mentor texts, establishing success criteria, etc.	**Whole Class** Active participation in lesson and various activities to build foundational knowledge.
10–20 minutes	**Purposeful Practice Time (round 1)**	
	Teacher	Students
	Small-Group Instruction Working with a small group of students based on focus for instruction (composition and/or word skills).	**Purposeful Practice Time** **Group 1:** Independent Reading **Group 2:** Partner Reading **Group 3:** Independent Composing **Group 4:** Peer Sharing

15–30 minutes	Direct Instruction: Comprehension and Fluency	
	Teacher	Students
	Comprehension and/or Fluency Teaching students how to engage with texts by reading aloud, explicitly teaching decoding and fluency strategies, posing critical thinking questions, exploring diverse world views and perspectives, etc.	**Whole Class** Active participation in lesson and various activities to build background knowledge.
10–20 minutes	Purposeful Practice Time (round 2)	
	Teacher	Students
	Small-Group Instruction Working with a small group of students based on focus for instruction (comprehension, fluency, and/or decoding skills).	**Purposeful Practice Time** **Group 1:** Responding to Texts **Group 2:** Responding to Texts **Group 3:** Peer Sharing **Group 4:** Independent Composing

Tracking Purposeful Practice Time

While all other elements remain the same on the following day, the tasks that students complete during Purposeful Practice Time will begin to rotate. Students are divided into groups as an organizational strategy. They don't complete all their activities as a group; rather, each group is assigned a different task (for example, Group 1 works on Independent Reading while Group 2 has Technology Time). While some tasks, such as Peer Sharing, require collaboration, Word Skills and Independent Reading and Composing require students to work independently.

A class tracking board can be very useful in organizing the various tasks and keeping track as elements of the literacy block are added. Educators can enlarge the template on page 36 and move copies of the routine cards on page 37 around on the tracking board.

When you introduce students to Purposeful Practice Time, they must take a great deal of responsibility for tracking their tasks. A tracking board can provide visual reminders of what students need to be doing during their independent and collaborative work time. For example, students in Group 1 are able to see that on the first day they work on their Independent Reading and then Respond to Texts, either by completing a comprehension task on a text of choice or a text the whole class has engaged in together. By moving the tasks down one spot on the tracking board, you can assign tasks for the following day. The removal of the teacher from the tracking board and the intentional sequencing of tasks allows flexibility of groupings. (More on this in Chapters 4 and 6.)

Three sequential days are given here, showing how each group would rotate through the various tasks. Your tracking boards might look something like this:

SAMPLE TRACKING BOARD: DAY 1

Group	First I will …	Then I will …
Group 1	Independent Reading	Responding to Texts
Group 2	Partner Reading	Responding to Texts
Group 3	Independent Composing	Peer Sharing
Group 4	Peer Sharing/Brainstorming	Independent Composing

By rotating the tasks down one cell every day, the individual task assignments are adjusted for the following day.

SAMPLE TRACKING BOARD: DAY 2

Group	First I will …	Then I will …
Group 1	Peer Sharing/Brainstorming	Independent Composing
Group 2	Independent Reading	Responding to Texts

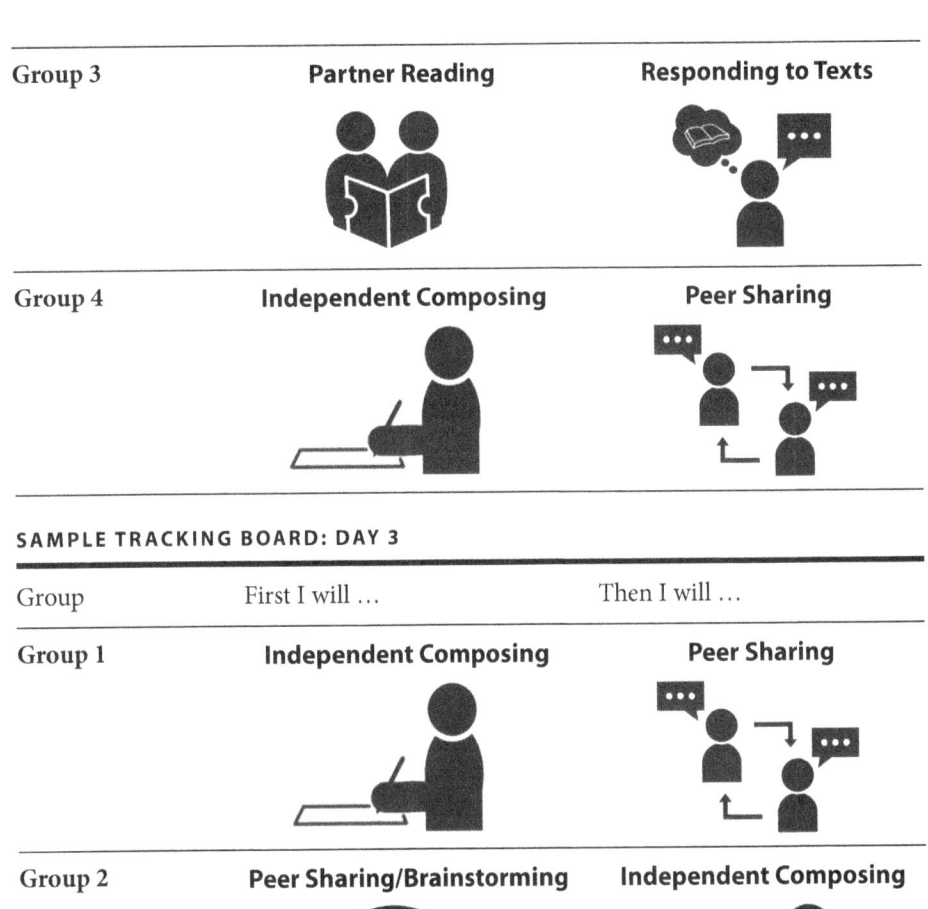

Building in Accountability

By creating tasks that are mainly independent, teachers are able to work through the routine while being responsive and flexible in their small-group instruction. It will be important for educators to develop tasks that are authentic and purposeful for engagement in order to ensure we are being culturally responsive and relevant. In using our deep knowledge of our learners, educators will be better able to support students in applying transferable skills by providing opportunities for cross-curricular learning that build upon the collective knowledge of the class. Educators also have the opportunity to develop students' media and digital literacy skills through the use of technology when they design independent activities and purposeful practice tasks for their students.

Educators must also consider the assessment demands of the literacy tasks and how students can apply their feedback in a timely manner. You do not need to mark everything! These purposeful practice tasks and activities are meant to be exactly that: time for students to engage in composition/comprehension tasks to develop their skills before applying them in a formal assessment/evaluation opportunity. The assessment demands of these tasks should rather focus on the teacher's ability to provide timely feedback so students can most effectively build their skills.

As the literacy block continues to develop, it becomes possible to add the elements that provide opportunities for ongoing monitoring of students' learning during their independent work times. Through these elements, teachers can assess students' language comprehension, track the texts students are engaging with, and provide support and practice for students in specific learning areas. Teachers can use direct-instruction times to introduce students to additional elements as they are added to the literacy routine. These elements could include word skills, transcription practice, and technology (if possible).

The following student tracking charts might be helpful as they continue to build Purposeful Practice Time. The optional Groups 5 and 6 allow for students to add word-skills activities, transcription practice (typing or cursive-writing tasks), and technology-based tasks that build in explicit opportunities for cross-curricular application of literacy skills.

SAMPLE TRACKING BOARD: DAY 1

Group	First I will …	Then I will …
Group 1	**Independent Reading**	**Responding to Texts**
Group 2	**Partner Reading**	**Responding to Texts**
Group 3	**Words Skills**	**Transcription Practice**

Group 4	Independent Composing	Peer Sharing

Group 5	Peer Sharing/Brainstorming	Independent Composing

Group 6	Technology Time: Blended Learning Tasks	

SAMPLE TRACKING BOARD: DAY 2

Group	First I will …	Then I will …
Group 1	Technology Time: Blended Learning Tasks	
Group 2	Independent Reading	Responding to Texts
Group 3	Partner Reading	Responding to Texts
Group 4	Words Skills	Transcription Practice

The Building Blocks 31

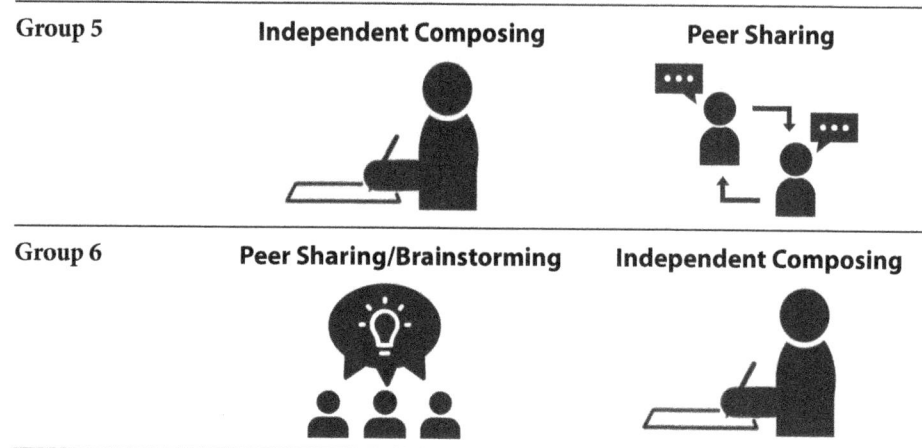

Again, when tasks are rotated down one position, the students can continue to transfer their learning the following day. For example, students who met for partner reading and then worked on a responding to texts task will have an opportunity the following day to read/listen independently and transfer this learning to their independent reading/listening texts. Students who spent time on Day 1 brainstorming or sharing writing goals and ideas with their peers and then composing independently will have time the following day to revisit their writing and then have an opportunity to share this writing with their peers. The new groups working on word skills, transcription, and technology will have the opportunity to build specific skills related to comprehension and composition. As well, the students working on technology will realistically need the entire Purposeful Practice Time in order to access and best utilize the available technology tools. It is important to remember that all learning should be authentic and purposeful. These added activities should never be used as a "busy" station for students, but rather be directly connected to the work of the class.

Building Blocks in Place

Here is the final literacy block:

THE LITERACY BLOCK

Approximate time	Literacy Activity	
5–10 minutes	**Bell Work** (word-skills activities to allow for transition time)	
15–30 minutes	**Direct Instruction: Composition and Word Skills**	
	Teacher	Students
	Composition and/or Word Skills Teaching students various composition or word skills competencies through explicit instruction, modelling, examination of mentor texts, establishing success criteria, etc.	**Whole Class** Active participation in lesson and various activities to build foundational knowledge.

30–40 minutes (divided into two 15–20 minute work times)	**Purposeful Practice Time (round 1)**	
	Teacher	Students
	Small-Group Instruction Working with a small group of students based on focus for instruction (composition and/or word skills).	**Purposeful Practice Time** **Group 1:** Independent Reading **Group 2:** Partner Reading **Group 3:** Word Skills **Group 4:** Peer Sharing **Group 5:** Independent Composing **Group 6:** Technology Time
	Purposeful Practice Time (round 2)	
	Teacher	Students
	Small-Group Instruction Working with a small group of students based on focus for instruction (comprehension, fluency, and/or decoding skills).	**Purposeful Practice Time** **Group 1:** Responding to Texts **Group 2:** Responding to Texts **Group 3:** Transcription Practice **Group 4:** Independent Composing **Group 5:** Peer Sharing **Group 6:** Technology Time
15–30 minutes	**Direct Instruction: Comprehension and Fluency**	
	Teacher	Students
	Comprehension and/or Fluency Teaching students how to engage with texts by reading aloud, explicitly teaching decoding and fluency strategies, posing critical thinking questions, exploring diverse world views and perspectives, etc.	**Whole Class** Active participation in lesson and various activities to build background knowledge.

Additionally, time for Transition Activities (often referred to as Bell Work) has also been added as another opportunity for students to work on word skills while they transition into the classroom and prepare for whole-class learning. In order to maximize instructional time, I prefer to utilize Bell Work time for word-skills activities to allow all students to be engaged and to make intentionally planning for differentiation easier.

At this point, all the elements of the literacy block are firmly in place. By introducing students to each element in turn and taking time to build a literacy block, you set the stage for effective literacy instruction. You might find the following chart, "Sample Timeline for Introduction of Elements of the Literacy Block," helpful when you plan daily and weekly literacy instruction.

SAMPLE TIMELINE FOR INTRODUCTION OF ELEMENTS OF THE LITERACY BLOCK

Approximate timeline	Elements of the Literacy Block
Week 1	- Begin by bookending the literacy block with two distinct times for direct instruction, beginning with Composition Time and ending with Comprehension Time.
Weeks 2–3	- Add times for independent practice of composition and comprehension activities, gradually increasing the time that students spend engaged in each task. - In week 3 (at the earliest), begin to use independent practice time to meet with individual students for reading assessments (screeners) or initial observations.
Weeks 4–6	- Continue to complete assessments for learning (e.g., diagnostic decoding assessments) to collect assessment data to support instructional foci for small-group instruction. - Introduce students to Bell Work (transition activities utilizing word skills) to build a routine for transitioning into class time from a structured break such as recess or lunch time. - Introduce students to the tracking board, including literacy tasks to be completed during simplified Purposeful Practice Time (with tasks that have been introduced: independent and partner reading, responding to texts, independent composing, peer sharing, word skills). - Form initial instructional groupings and begin to use Purposeful Practice Time to meet with groups for small-group targeted instruction and intervention. - Use whole-class direct instruction time to introduce students to tasks and expectations for responding to texts, peer sharing, and word skills. At this point, it is best to keep it simple and include a limited selection of responding to texts and word-skills tasks in order to support students in building their stamina for independent work time.
Week 7+	- Add elements to the Purposeful Practice Time tracking board (transcription practice activities and simple technology tasks), ensuring that students transition from one learning task to another in a way that intentionally connects independent practice to small-group and peer-sharing activities. For example, independent reading and responding to texts follows partner reading so students have had time for fluency practice with a peer before reading or listening to reading on their own. - Have students rotate through at least three cycles per week, completing at least two activities a day. In a weekly cycle, Mondays can be set-up days to facilitate longer whole-class lessons and shared composition or comprehension tasks within the gradual release of responsibility, while Fridays can be "flex Fridays" to build in catch-up time for students and additional lesson time. A bonus of this organization is that when you inevitably miss a Monday or Friday for a holiday, you can still maintain your cycle of tasks.

	• Continue to revisit routines and expectations for all learning times, ensuring that students have opportunities to select word-skills activities, texts, as well as composition topics that interest them.
Throughout the year	• Continue to use direct-instruction times to introduce students to new learning tasks and to add to the selection of responding-to-texts activities, composition prompts, and technology assignments. • Revisit instructional groupings frequently and form new groups as needed. Purposeful Practice Time groupings can change as necessary for classroom management (say, once a month) and your small-group instructional groupings will change and be responsive to student progress. For example, if one student in the group has met the desired learning outcome from the instruction, they no longer need to meet with that group when they come together for targeted instruction. Your groupings should always be tied to your focus for instruction, meeting students' specific needs and interests.

Tracking Board

Group	First I will …	Then I will …
Group 1		
Group 2		
Group 3		
Group 4		
Group 5		
Group 6		

Routine Cards

Independent Reading	Independent Composing
Partner Reading	Peer Sharing/Brainstorming
Responding to Texts	Peer Sharing
Word Skills	Transcription Practice
Tech Time	

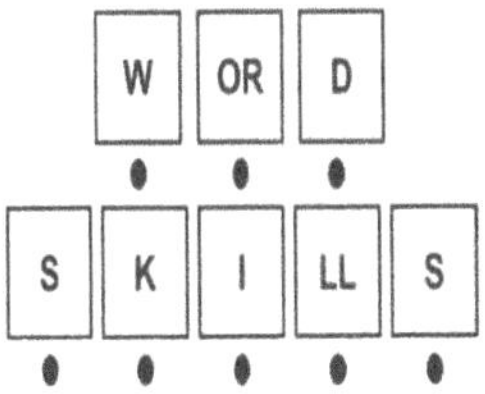

3

Composition: Writing, Speaking, Creating

As the students gather as a group, the teacher begins by reminding them about the mentor texts they have engaged in together over the last several days. They were able to watch a short video, look at a picture book, and read a small sample of a novel as a class. She asks them to recall some of the features that make them strong samples of work. The students take a few minutes to turn and talk with their talk-partners, recalling details of the sample mentor texts. The teacher then takes an opportunity to reexamine parts to which she wants to draw students' attention to highlight the particular skill or strategy, such as dialogue, that may be the focus for instruction. After a few moments, the teacher invites students to share their thinking with the whole group. One student remembers that the video's dialogue shows the relationship between the two characters, another recalls that the picture book makes each character sound different, and another describes the way Mia expresses herself to show that she is a Chinese immigrant.

The teacher captures the students' ideas and lists the things that make the dialogue work in each example:

- The dialogue shows what characters are feeling.
- The dialogue makes each character sound unique.
- The dialogue shows relationships (or hierarchy) between characters.
- The dialogue reveals information about plot.
- The dialogue uses humour.
- The dialogue shows different perspectives.
- The authors use quotation marks (or don't) to show when characters are speaking.

After reading the story aloud, the teacher asks the students to comment on the things they noticed about it. As a class, they engage in a rich conversation about what is done well and what may be missing from the examples of dialogue. The students determine that dialogue is a conversation between two or more people and can help them hear how characters express themselves, build relationships, and move a story forward.

Students are then invited to write a telephone conversation between two people. To prepare, they find their talk-partners and have a conversation about one of several scenarios the teacher has shared with the class. It is important to give students a topic or scenario to write about to support them in the initial thinking phase so they can move quickly to the composition task with their partner.

The pairs of students disperse into the classroom: some at desks, some sprawled on the floor, and others choosing to sit at the conference table. Each pair chooses a scenario. After talking it through, they begin to write a dialogue that clearly articulates the perspectives of the people talking on the phone. Rich conversations erupt and fill the classroom with engaging, purposeful talk.

After a while, the students return together as a class. When they are invited, the students eagerly share their conversations. The teacher selects an example from a group (already discussed with that group) or one that she has previously created and shares the written dialogue with the class either on chart paper or using a doc-cam. At this point, she is able to work with the class directly to teach the role of quotation marks in dialogue writing and explicitly point out or correct the essential rules for formatting dialogue.

The class pauses to admire their handiwork and is then invited to move into Purposeful Practice Time as outlined on the board. As a part of the independent composition time, students are invited to revise their own conversations, putting the rules they have just reviewed into action. The teacher reminds the students of their collective goal to create authentic conversations that communicate one of the initial scenarios shared with the class. She also asks students to consider what else could be added to (or removed from) their current work to make sure their ideas are clear.

Students scramble and hurry to dive into their tasks and activities while the teacher finds the opportunity to pull a small-group for intentional and targeted support with any number of literacy skills.

Author's Note

The inspiration for this example is in Larry Swartz's book *Write to Read: Ready-to-use classroom lessons that explore the ABCs of writing*, specifically his activity titled "Dialogue." The movie clip I considered for this task was from the movie *Zootopia*. Students could watch a short clip from the movie (approximately two minutes) when the character Judy Hopps is "hustling" Nick Wilde (for tax evasion) to gather information for a case she is covering. This is a pivotal scene that cleverly uses dialogue to reveal their personalities and the dynamic of their budding (and initially adversarial) relationship. I also considered the picture book *It's a Book*, by Lane Smith, for this task. This text uses minimal dialogue to create humor and share the message of the story. The witty exchanges between Donkey and Monkey effectively highlight the simple joys of a physical book versus digital devices. Their contrasting perspectives provide rich examples of dialogue revealing character and a generational tech gap. Finally, the novel I considered for this task was *Front Desk* by Kelly Yang. It features exceptional dialogue central to the story. Mia Tang's conversations with hotel guests, her parents, and friends effectively highlight cultural nuances and the immigrant experience. Her clever observations and her parents' still-developing English skills provide rich examples revealing character and cultural background.

The Composition Process

Composing, and writing specifically, is a complex process. The Composition Time you have carved out of the literacy block will give you an opportunity to provide students with direct instruction to help them learn the necessary skills for composing text. This time can be used for developing the building blocks for all writing (sentences!); modelling new forms of composition; exploring mentor texts and determining success criteria; providing grammar lessons or instruction on parts of speech or word patterns within curriculum-driven content; teaching students how to select topics for composition, to brainstorm, and to organize their ideas; developing a personal voice; and much more.

At this point, it is important to make a distinction between writing and composition. Simply put, writing is a specific set of skills under the umbrella of composition. Composition includes a variety of expressive language skills, such as writing, speaking, and creating, that students can use to communicate their ideas. By highlighting the various ways that students can express themselves, teachers are better equipped to differentiate tasks to suit students' needs while still meeting curriculum expectations. Many expectations and skills associated with composition do not explicitly require students to put their ideas down in writing as they are not exclusively tied to written work.

Students learn to express ideas and create texts by applying their knowledge of oral language (Ontario Ministry of Education, 2023). Unlike oral language, written language is a human invention and requires "rewiring" of the brain. (More on this in Chapter 5.) As a result of this "rewiring," explicit and systematic methods of instruction will best meet the needs of all students. Although in the past (and somewhat in the present) most academic researchers seemingly paid far more attention to reading than writing, the same evidence-based methods of instruction will apply to writing as it does to reading. Students develop the competencies and confidence to communicate clearly with an audience by applying their oral language skills through explicit instruction that is systematic and follows a logical sequence.

In reading instruction, we do not merely give our students a book and say, "Read this." Rather, we scaffold our receptive language instruction intentionally and build upon skills in reasonable steps toward skilled reading (decoding and comprehension). Expressive language should be taught in a similar manner, while considering the variety of skills students must employ to become effective communicators. Educators therefore must consider composition of all media, forms, and genres within expressive language skills, such as writing, speaking, and creating. Language instruction is more than just traditional reading, writing, and speaking skills. The process involves engaging multiple senses and modalities to make sense of text, including visual (seeing), aural (hearing), oral (speaking), gestural (body language), and spatial (awareness of space). When we consider the interaction and combination of these senses and modalities, we are better able to prepare students to receive, understand, represent, and communicate information and ideas.

Now more than ever, students are being bombarded with texts in many different modes: written, oral, visual, audio, and multimodal texts from various cultural communities and from print and digital environments. Therefore, teachers must employ a variety of teaching methods to meet the ever-changing needs of the students in front of them. Composition Time is a perfect opportunity to introduce students to the various purposes for composition, explore potential audiences, and introduce written and other forms of expressive language in a range of formats. This time allows teachers to provide direct instruction using mentor texts (such as published pieces), student exemplars, or modelled pieces of writing to help students acquire the knowledge necessary to use their independent Composition Time in a focused, productive way. As students are introduced to different expressive competencies and foundational skills that are the building blocks of written language, they can apply them during Purposeful Practice

Time. In this way, they can test the skills they are learning with their own composing and receive immediate feedback on their progress.

Through direct instruction, teachers provide the framework for students to explore composing through their independent Composition Time. The direct-instruction Composition Time should be intentionally connected to the work that students are doing during their Purposeful Practice Time. In this way, students are being provided regular times to practice the skills that are explicitly taught through the lessons. This daily instructional time provides teachers with an opportunity to provide whole-class instruction (and possibly whole-class feedback), while the independent practice time provides the opportunity to meet for small-group instruction to target building of specific skills.

Direct Instruction in Composition: Writing

Hochman, Wexler, and Maloney (2025) state that "the problem is not that students are incapable of learning to write well. Rather the problem is that many schools haven't been teaching students how to write. Teachers may assign writing, but they may not know how to explicitly teach it in a careful sequence of logical steps" (p. 2). This is not to say that you are the problem! Most teacher-training programs don't include this instruction as it has long been assumed that if students read and write enough, they will simply pick up the skills they need to be proficient. However, at the end of the day, the evidence-based research does not support this notion.

During direct-instruction Composition Time, teachers can model the numerous skills that good writing and composition encompasses. Research indicates that teachers need to provide clear, coherent, and evidence-based instruction when teaching writing, no matter the subject or grade level (Hochman, Wexler, & Maloney, 2025). Through this whole-class time, teachers can explicitly teach a range of skills associated with proficient writing. It can be used to explore different text forms and purposes, to give focused instruction on the various components of the writing process, to provide an opportunity to help students gain insights into the craft of writing, including voice and style, or to provide a time to brainstorm and share potential topics or ideas for composition.

MODELLING

Teacher modelling is a powerful tool for young writers. In the same way that modelled reading allows us to explicitly share the processes we use when reading, modelled writing allows us to demonstrate the strategies we use as writers: how we overcome the challenges in getting our thoughts down in writing. Modelled writing helps students develop an understanding of not only the elements of writing, but also the craft of writing. Through this process, they can see the ways in which a good writer organizes ideas, experiments with words, and uses their writer's voice in different ways for various purposes and forms of writing.

A piece of writing created through teacher modelling can also be used as a mentor text from which the students can construct success criteria. Students can identify the various text features, skills, and strategies used throughout the piece. They can record their observations on sticky notes and attach them to the modelled piece, or you might choose to highlight the areas of the writing that demonstrate specific skills the students need to notice. As students identify the important elements of the piece, you can use their observations to form the basis for the success criteria. (More on this in Chapter 8: *Feedback and Assessment*.)

As you model, you can draw the students' attention to various elements important to their own writing. As the success criteria are constructed, you can discuss which strategies were used to get the desired results and what the writer was thinking while crafting the piece. This insight into a writer's mind helps young authors understand that writing is the result of an internal dialogue and a reflective thought process the writer uses to find just the right word or phrase, and to organize ideas so that they are clear to the reader.

As any author will tell you, writing is a messy process. It includes brainstorming, drafting, and lots and lots of revision. Through direct instruction, students not only explore mentor texts that are copy perfect, but they also have an opportunity to witness the down-and-dirty craft of creating a piece of writing. The teacher can serve as a writer, modelling the various forms of writing as well as the process of writing. When students understand the thinking processes associated with writing, they are better able to apply these strategies to their own writing. This is significant for every teacher's practice as "writing isn't just a skill. Writing instruction can also be a powerful tool for teaching content" (Hochman, Wexler, & Maloney, 2025, p. 279).

Still, the curriculum tells us where our students should end up, so the real question for teachers is how we get them there. For teachers to implement instruction or model writing that focuses on students' development and targets their areas of need, educators must be able to break down the composition process and understand the various components of skilled writing. This provides the framework that independent composition time will build on, allowing for teachers to engage in small-group instruction where they can provide students with timely and targeted feedback.

SKILLED WRITING AS AN OUTCOME

> See Chapter 5 for more information on Scarborough's Reading Rope.

As we have been engaging with the Science of Reading, many educators have become familiar with the Reading Rope. Just as Hollis Scarborough created the Reading Rope model, Joan Sedita (2019) suggests a similar model for writing, the Writing Rope, that identifies the various components of skilled writing.

This rope metaphor demonstrates the five "strands" that lead students to fluent, skilled writing, including critical thinking, syntax, text structure, writing craft, and transcription, which are summarized below.

Critical Thinking: Critical thinking is vital to composition as students think deeply about their message and work to determine what they want to communicate to their audience. If they're writing to inform or persuade, they need to engage their comprehension skills to gather and analyze the information they want to share. Teachers should provide direct instruction in brainstorming strategies, taking notes from different sources, and using graphic organizers to plan and organize content for composition. Students also need to build an understanding that the writing process is not linear. How many times has a student said, "I'm done!" while you know there is much more work to do? It is important for teachers to explicitly model the movement back and forth between steps in the drafting and revision process to provide direct instruction for students on how to revise and edit their work. The critical thinking required of writers as they move toward final drafts of their work is extensive. Students need to explicitly see that writers move between and through the steps of the writing process several times and for different purposes before a piece of work is published.

Syntax: As Sedita (2019) states, "*syntax* is the study and understanding of grammar—the system and arrangement of words, phrases and clauses that make up a sentence" (p. 2). Before students can put together a well-crafted paragraph, report, or essay, they first need to be able to write a complete sentence. This begins by listening to spoken language, reading, or listening to people read to develop the correct use of words in sentences and the relationships between them. From there, students learn to efficiently process sentence structure to build comprehension and to communicate through composition. Therefore, educators need to provide direct instruction on the fundamentals of sentence construction, elaboration, and combining.

Text Structure: Students learn to read and write effectively by understanding text structure, specifically in written language. Since written language is a human invention that has developed over time, it is vital for students to grasp several levels of text structure in order to contribute to the "rewiring" of their brains. Explicit and systematic instruction of these layers has a significant impact on comprehension and composition and includes the following: genre-specific organization, such as informational reports written with a clear beginning, middle, and end; paragraph construction, specifically focused on chunking text into units containing a main idea and supporting details; patterns of organization, such as sequencing, cause/effect, and compare/contrast; and transitional language used to tie together sentences, paragraphs, and sections of writing.

Writing Craft: This aspect of writing instruction focuses on students' intentional use of language and stylistic elements, such as word choice, literary devices, and awareness of purpose and audience. This "craft" is often how students develop their personal writer's voice. They require direct instruction and modelling of how to select and place specific words and vocabulary to intentionally communicate meaning to their audience. Additionally, students learn how to use various literary devices, including elements (such as plot, setting, and characters) and techniques (such as emphasis, repetition, and figurative language devices). Finally, as outlined in Chapter 2, students need to learn to maintain a keen awareness of their purpose and audience for writing, as this will influence the decisions they make, from word choice to the length and style of a written composition.

Transcription: This strand addresses the foundational skills of spelling and handwriting (or keyboarding) that students need to develop to become fluent writers. Becoming fluent in spelling and handwriting/keyboarding is like learning to decode: it enables students to focus their cognitive energy on the other aspects of skilled writing as they more efficiently manage the mechanics of writing.

With a greater understanding of the specific skills students need to learn to become proficient, fluent writers, teachers are better equipped to plan for instruction that is both meaningful and meets the needs of the students in front of them. When we consider whole-class instruction during Composition Time, it is not simply a time to deliver content. It is an opportunity for teachers to better understand student learning and growth. In gathering this crucial information, we can intentionally target small-group instruction to support students who need interventions with specific skills and build enrichment for those honing their skills.

> **The Power of Talk**
>
> During Composition Time, students should have frequent opportunities to engage in conversations with each other. This talk can take the form of examining mentor texts in order to determine success criteria, brainstorming collaboratively, or sharing a piece of work and giving or receiving feedback with their peers. When students are given time to think about their ideas and have an opportunity to share them orally, they meet with greater success in writing them down. Using whole-class Composition Time as a vehicle for teaching leads students to determine the purpose and audience for their pieces, to understand forms of composition, and to share their thinking aloud. These skills will have a significant impact on students' independent composition during Purposeful Practice Time. Students will be more apt to use their time productively, having already had time to think about potential ideas.

Exploring Purpose and Audience

When we compose, we do so for a variety of purposes. We might write a letter to a friend, create an invitation to an event, e-mail a recipe, record a podcast to share a book review, or—most dreaded—write a report card to share information with parents. In our lives, we've had to write for a number of different reasons and recognize, perhaps without giving it much conscious thought, the purpose and audience of each form. However, most forms of composition can be reflected in the following purposes: to inform, to persuade, to reflect, or to entertain. We also compose for different audiences: we might write an email to a colleague, create a podcast for personal and shared reflection, jot down a to-do list for a spouse, or compose a presentation for a committee we participate in. When we combine the purpose of composition with the intended audience, we can adjust the form accordingly. For example, we might be asked to write a letter to someone in order to convince them of something. In this light, we would combine the purpose (to convince someone) with the audience (recipient of the letter) to determine the form the writing should take (a persuasive letter).

After they focus on specific purposes of composition and build an awareness of the audience, students can use this information to determine the form and voice their composition should take. When we compose to inform, we could record a procedure in a how-to video; when we compose to persuade, we might write a paragraph, letter, or essay; when we compose to reflect, we might create a visual journal or record a podcast with our thoughts; when we compose to entertain, we might choose to write a narrative or a script for a play we would like to see performed. All of these forms align with how students are learning to use effective and appropriate language to establish their voice, point of view, and perspectives, and to convey their intended message. Educators can also help students determine the form their composition needs to take by teaching them to balance the purpose and the audience for each task while also examining the availability of the resources they need for any given format.

For each type of composition, you will find a variety of tools: question prompts to get students to think and reflect, graphic organizers to help students plan their composition, and sample learning goals and success criteria that will help students know what they need to demonstrate to create compositions that meet curriculum expectations.

Using Writing Prompts

Hmm … what should I write about?

This is a tough question for children and adults alike. Just getting started is often the hardest part. The prospect of deciding on a topic, brainstorming ideas, formulating a plan, and organizing information can sometimes be enough to give even the most confident creator a block. While we can't teach students to be inspired, we can set the stage for inspiration to happen. What is inspiration? Inspiration is the explosion in our mind that starts our creativity flowing. How can we help students find their own inspiration? Providing meaningful tasks and topics while also allowing students to have choice in the mode they use to compose (writing, speaking, or creating) can help students get over the block that sometimes comes with writing.

Artifact Box as Inspiration

Students benefit from experiential learning. In order to write or create, they need sufficient background knowledge. They need to be able to draw on their prior experiences to create vibrant mental images for their readers or a convincing argument from a certain perspective. All students bring a wealth of personal experiences, opinions, and perspectives to each classroom. However, they might not be able to recall certain details at a moment's notice. They might forget specific details or be unable to recall elements that could help to build a realistic image in their audience's mind.

An Artifact Box can help students use tangible objects as a way to connect to their prior experiences and unlock their creativity. This box would contain a number of different items that students can use as a source of inspiration. What would happen if students discovered an old key in the Artifact Box? They could think of a wide range of questions: Where did it come from? What does it unlock? What secret is it hiding? How can we find the lock it opens? Are there any clues on the key that might help us discover what it unlocks? Who owns the treasure behind the lock? Should we keep it a secret, and why or why not?

Other ideas for an Artifact Box:

- Neighborhood poster (wanted ad, lost pet, etc.)
- Old lamp, jar, or container
- Leaf (or other artifact from nature)
- Old road map
- Torn sports jersey
- Used airline boarding pass
- Family portrait
- Signed baseball card
- Business card with website
- Old toys or stuffed animals
- Tools
- Costume jewellery

> During Composition Time, students are introduced to different items to be placed in the Artifact Box or share items they have contributed for the class. Students might need time to explore the items and think about the stories they hold. These discussions can take place during Composition Time or even when students participate in peer sharing during Purposeful Practice Time. The teacher might choose to model writing using an artifact as a source of inspiration. Providing time for students to explore the Artifact Box before and during Purposeful Practice Time can help those who are struggling with writer's block to find a new and creative source of inspiration.

One strategy for introducing students to different topic ideas is to have them use Composition Time to explore different prompts. For example, if students are learning how to compose narratives, you could ask them to sit with a talk-partner. Begin by sharing one of the prompts (found on pages 54–56) with the whole class. For example, the Entertaining Ideas are suitable prompts for students to use when composing narratives or stories. After reading the prompt, allow at least 20–30 seconds for students to do some independent thinking. Then have them take a few minutes to share their ideas with their talk-partners. During this pre-writing discussion, students can be presented with different aspects of the narrative to think and talk about; for example, you might say, "For the next prompt, think about the setting: where would a story like this take place?" or "When I read the prompt, consider if there will be a conflict in the story: how would the problem be created?" or "After listening to the prompt, think about who might be involved in the story: what characters will need to be developed?"

Scaffolding the students' writing by allowing them time to think and talk before composing will help them select topics, gather ideas, and organize their thinking to optimize their Purposeful Practice Time. If students have been introduced to a variety of prompts and have had an opportunity to think about them, they will be less likely to face the dreaded writer's block during their independent composing time.

Prompts can help students generate ideas for their writing. However, they should never be used to limit students' creativity. It is vital for educators to consider some of the following questions when generating or selecting prompts to spark students' thinking:

- Whose perspectives are being advanced or highlighted through topic choices?
- Whose voices are missing from the topic or prompt choices presented?
- How do these prompts shed light or raise awareness of inequality and oppression?
- Are these prompts rooted in a colonial worldview, or do they perpetuate biased representations of specific groups (cultural, racial, gender, etc.)?
- What potential do these topic choices or prompts have to demonstrate the diversity of our community?
- How are students encouraged to critically evaluate topics or prompts for their potential bias, inaccuracies, or incomplete information?
- How can I create meaningful and authentic opportunities for student voice and choice within topic or prompt selection in our learning environment?

Students should be encouraged to use prompts to inspire their own writing, creating, and thinking about additional potential topics for composition. Students can add to the existing bank of prompts or collect pictures and other artifacts to serve as catalysts for creativity. The more ideas students contribute, the more authentic and relevant their compositions will be. The prompts included in this book are broad and general, to reach as wide an audience as possible; they are meant to be suggestions and supports. Each class will have different interests, which should be reflected in the topics generated for them. As teachers are the experts on their own students, they should select the prompts they think might best inspire them and then work with them to brainstorm and create additional composition ideas. The more time we invest in helping students find their own topics, ideas, and inspiration, the more engaged they will be in the composition process.

Inspiration is found through choice—if students have an opportunity to browse through different ideas, they can select one they are passionate about or that helps them formulate their own ideas. Select the topics that best support the type of instruction taking place during Composition Time. You might decide to use ideas from Recall and Reflect when teaching students how to develop recounts, or possibly from Inform Me! when teaching students about reporting on a topic; you might find the ideas in HOT Topics (higher-order thinking) perfect for expositions, and the Entertaining Ideas could help when students are crafting narratives or other creative pieces that relate to the arts curriculum.

While this book provides a number of prompts, nothing replaces brainstorming with your students. They bring a wealth of experiences, knowledge, interests, and opinions to the classroom, so consider them as a foundation for new composition ideas. Involve students in the creation of topics that can be added to their choices to consider when composing their ideas.

For simplicity's sake, consider creating a space in the classroom where the ideas can be kept. You might create an Inspiration Box and place the prompts on recipe cards sorted into different sections; you might create a system where the ideas are housed in pockets stapled to a bulletin board. With younger students, you could introduce one idea (or two at the most) during the Composition Time and allow them to brainstorm with their talk-partners, so that when they choose a topic they will already have had an opportunity to think and talk about the ideas they would like to use in their composition. With older students, consider introducing three or four ideas at a time and providing them with some time to think and talk with their talk-partners about which one(s) they might consider when working on composing. Students can tuck cards they find interesting into their writing books to serve as inspiration during their independent composing time. When you introduce students to ideas during the whole-class Composition Time, they are well prepared for their independent composing time. They can then use their Purposeful Practice Time to actually write, record, or create, knowing they have already taken the time to think and talk about their ideas.

PURPOSE: TO REFLECT

Composing to reflect allows the student time to recount various events and consider their significance. This composition can take the form of writing in a journal or diary, recording a personal recount in a podcast, or creating a series of artistic pieces (such as a sequence of collages or a song with multiple verses) to represent significant feelings or emotions from an experience. Typically, students present nonfiction information about a personal experience in sequential order; that is, they describe events in the order that they happened.

You might find the following list of questions helpful when you introduce students to reflective composition, either during Composition Time or in small-group instructional conferences. These questions might help students generate or reflect on their ideas for composition:

- What do you want your audience to know about this experience?
- How did you feel about it?
- What words or images will you include to help the audience understand your thoughts and feelings?
- How can you use sequencing words (e.g., *first, then, finally*) to organize your ideas?
- Did you learn an important lesson through this event?
- What do you want your audience to continue thinking about after they engage with your text?
- Are there parts that you can describe vividly?
- How can you use your five senses to describe the event?
- How do you want your audience to feel after they engage with your text?
- What words or images can you use to help give your audience a good mental image of the event you are describing?
- Which parts are the most important? Are there any irrelevant parts that you could leave out?
- Are any parts more important than others? How will you draw your audience's attention to these parts?

A Caution about Privacy

The audience for a journal can be public or private. When we write to reflect, we might be writing to share our personal experiences with others or to help ourselves better understand the things that happen in our lives. There are times when keeping a journal can help us work through different events in our lives; the value of these journals comes from the process of writing, not the product that is derived. Some people find this kind of journaling therapeutic, as it helps them gain a better understanding of their own thinking. However, this kind of reflective writing should be kept private and used only for the purpose of "thinking through writing." If students choose to keep personal journals at home, these writings need to be respected as private personal reflections. This should be clearly communicated to students since they may also share sensitive information that we would have a duty to report. Whether we are reading students' reflections or not needs to be communicated so our duty to report does not come into question.

In addition, unfortunately there have been times students have mistaken various public forums as appropriate places to post their private personal reflections. Just as we need to encourage students to have a safe private forum to reflect on their own lives, we also need to help them develop an awareness of which reflections are best kept private, which can be shared with a select audience, and which are suitable for sharing publicly. With the ease of communicating digitally comes the need to help students distinguish between public and private information. Engaging in conversations about the intended audience for reflections is essential, so that students can develop an awareness of the differences between reflections that can be shared and those that should be kept private.

> We might ask students to reflect through a variety of forms or for different audiences. If we ask students to write for the purpose of reflecting, they need to know that their entries are not private and will be shared with an audience. This might alter the content and form of the composition.

You might find the graphic organizer "Compose to Reflect: Recall and Reflect" on page 54 helpful for students to use when they plan their reflections. "Composing Prompt Cards: Recall and Reflect" on pages 55–56 provides suggestions of topics that students can choose from. As with all composition activities, teachers should use the interests of each class to determine appropriate and engaging topics and ideas. The suggestions included in this book can help students get started, but teachers might find more value in brainstorming possible topics with their class.

PURPOSE: TO ENTERTAIN

People who compose for the purpose of entertaining typically use creativity and their imagination. This often takes the form of a narrative. A narrative tells a story and consists of the basic elements of a setting, characters, and a plot. As they create stories, students can develop their personal voice by experimenting with character development, use of sensory statements, creative word usage, and emotional cues. These all work together to develop an author's sense of style and ultimately their voice.

Voice-Building Strategies

Emotional Cues: Using emotional connections to build mood

Sensory Statements: Using the five senses to help readers create a mental image

Wordsmithing: Building vocabulary and promoting risk-taking with creative word use

Perspective: Understanding that the person telling the story is as important as the story itself

Character Development: Setting the stage for action by creating interesting characters with voices of their own

Style: Understanding how writing conventions, literary devices, and presentation techniques can be used to strengthen voice

(Donohue, 2011)

For the purpose of writing to entertain in particular, it is important to consider concepts such as authorship and Storywork. The term *Storywork* as it is widely understood and used today was coined by Q'um Q'um Xiiem, Dr. Jo-Ann Archibald (Stó:lō First Nation, British Columbia, Canada). Although there are other historical uses of the term, Dr. Archibald formalized it in her 2008 book *Indigenous Storywork: Educating the Heart, Mind, Body, and Spirit.* She shares that "by implication, the term storyWORK signals that Indigenous stories are to be taken seriously and that we as storytellers and storylisteners/readers/learners can work together to learn from and with these stories" (Archibald, n.d.).

As educators, we share a responsibility for Truth and Reconciliation and need to recognize that the creation of stories must move beyond the colonial narrative structure so common in our classrooms. When we teach only one method or story arc for composing a story, as a narrative with a set-up, conflict, challenge, climax, and resolution, we limit our students' understanding of what story is and what it can be. There are many different ways to engage in story as highlighted by the addition of First Nations, Inuit, Métis cultural texts to so many curricula. It is therefore vital for you to take up the call to acknowledge and follow Indigenous Storywork pedagogy and use the guiding principles Dr. Jo-Ann Archibald shares in her work to engage with stories.

You might find the following questions helpful when you introduce students to composing narrative during the Composition Time of the literacy block or when conferencing with students about their work:

- Are you creating a cultural text that needs to be shared with consideration for a particular pedagogy?
- Do you have the capacity to be an authentic author for the narrative you are sharing?
- How can you capture your audience's attention at the beginning?
- How can you create a mood of suspense/humor/joy/empathy through your work?
- Do you need any sequencing or time-order words (e.g., *first, then, after, finally*) to help clarify the sequence of events in your composition?
- Are there any words or sentences in your composition that support the audience in understanding how you (or the characters) are feeling?
- How can you include literary devices, such as foreshadowing, juxtaposition, or analogy, to help your audience's comprehension of your composition?
- How can you help the audience form a picture of your work in their mind?

By considering the many ways in which stories can be shared—a written narrative, an oral tradition, through graphics and other media—you can see that students can entertain audiences through sophisticated storylines in many ways. The graphic organizer "Compose to Entertain: A Story" on page 57 uses a chart structure to assist students in developing their ideas for common components of a narrative, allowing them to better transfer the ideas and organize their story in their form of choice. Pages 58–59 include "Composing Prompt Cards: Entertaining Ideas" that students might find helpful when they begin to develop their ideas. Place these prompts in a location that students can easily access during independent composing times.

PURPOSE: TO INFORM

Informative composition can take many different forms: it can be a procedural report, a recipe, an essay, a website, a radio commercial, a how-to video, or one of many other nonfiction texts. When an author composes to inform, the intent is to share information with the audience. The information the author shares might be a combination of personal experiences, prior knowledge, and facts learned through research or other sources.

When you teach students to create informative pieces, it makes sense to integrate many digital and critical literacy elements. This is a perfect time to introduce students to the challenges of evaluating the accuracy of information they encounter, especially if they are using online sources. They need to consider the source and to learn strategies for verifying the information. This could also be an appropriate time to introduce students to the importance of citing sources, the correct way to quote or share information, and the dangers of plagiarism.

Informational composition is likely what students will use the most as they progress through school and into post-secondary life. Therefore, students greatly benefit from developing their skills for informational composition as early as possible.

You might find these questions helpful when introducing students to informational composition during Composition Time or when conferencing with students during small-group instruction:

- How can you find information about your topic?
- How will you organize your information?
- What information can you group together? How will you organize the ideas so they flow in the most logical sequence?
- Do you know enough about the topic? If not, where will you find more information?
- How do you know if the information you have found is accurate and relevant? Can you trust your sources? How will you cite the sources that you used?
- Are you keeping a record of where you found your information?
- How can you capture your audience's attention at the beginning?
- What do you want your audience to continue thinking about after they have read, watched, or listened to your composition?
- Does all your information support your main idea? Is it all connected to your main idea? Is it relevant, specific, and accurate?
- Do any of your sources have conflicting information? How will you determine which source is most accurate?
- How might you share your work with your classmates?
- Is there someone you consider an expert on this subject who might be able to help you gather and organize your ideas?

The graphic organizer "Compose to Inform: Web Organizer" on page 60 and "Composing Prompt Cards: Inform Me!" on page 61 might help students generate ideas and collect information about their topics.

PURPOSE: TO PERSUADE

When we write to persuade, we are often attempting to convince the audience to change their beliefs in order to influence their actions through our text. To do this, we need to clearly state a point of view (often an opinion or a belief) and then defend or justify it in order to impact the audience emotionally and persuade them to make a change. The more logical our rationale, the more convincing our composition will be, which will lead, we hope, to the persuasion of our audience. When we ask students to form a judgment and then justify it, we are asking them to apply higher-order thinking skills. We are asking them to think critically and present a reasonable rationale to justify their ideas. In order to be critical thinkers, students need to be able to analyze information, evaluate possibilities, compare options, and effectively communicate their thinking. Critical thinking is not about having the correct answer, but instead about having a reasonable answer that can be justified. Students need to draw on their previous experiences and their prior knowledge in order to build a plausible answer. They need to be able to state an opinion and then justify their thinking by using evidence in the form of examples from their own lives, information they have read, or knowledge they have gained from reliable sources.

Composing to persuade demands that students state the idea and then justify their thinking. Students can demonstrate this skill in a variety of forms: writing a simple paragraph or a more-complex essay; creating a single poster or a series of works; recording a "soap-box" rant or a song that is meant to spark change. The principles remain the same: state an idea, opinion, or thesis and prove it using reliable sources of information (personal experiences, information, research if necessary).

You might use the following questions when introducing students to persuasive composition during Composition Time or when conferencing with students during small-group instruction:

- What is your opinion on the subject?
- How will you persuade others to agree with your point of view?
- What evidence can you use to support your opinion?
- How can you best organize your ideas so that they support your opinion?
- Are there words or phrases you can use to help clarify or express your opinion?
- What do you want the audience to think about after they have read, examined, or listened to your composition?
- What reliable source might you use to find out more information about this subject?
- How can you verify the reliability and accuracy of the sources you have consulted?
- Are there sources you should cite or reference in your work?
- Is there a possible counter-argument? How can you address it?

Students might find the graphic organizer "Compose to Persuade: Logic Table" on page 62 helpful when they plan their composition. Students of all ages can use similar strategies to build a persuasive argument; however, the complexity of the ideas and the sophistication of evidence will be reflective of students' age and development.

HOT TOPICS AND CROSS-CURRICULAR CONNECTIONS

Pages 63–66 contain "Composing Prompt Cards: HOT Topic" with suggested topics about which students might choose to persuade others. As with all composition activities, use the interests of each class to determine appropriate topics. The prompt cards can help get students started, but you might find more value in brainstorming possible topics with your class. Four boxes on page 66 are left blank for ideas created for your class.

When you create topics that elicit higher-order thinking through critical analysis, remember that students should be challenged to make a choice and then justify that choice. In younger grades, the choice could be as simple as, *Which animal do you think would make the best class pet?* Older students can be challenged with more sophisticated questions, such as, *If you could travel to any event in history, what would you choose to witness first-hand?*

Another avenue to consider when brainstorming topics with your class is to examine cross-curricular connections. To equip students with vital skills for navigating their world, you can intentionally embed overarching themes and skills within the literacy block. These cross-curricular elements can include areas such as environmental education, Indigenous education, digital literacy, financial literacy, and STEM education. For example, prompts in the younger grades could be as simple as *Why do we need to convince more people in our community to adopt a "reduce, reuse, recycle" mindset?* In older grades, we may wish to challenge students to consider ethical or moral dilemmas, such as, *Why is it ethically important to conserve water, even in areas with an abundant supply?*

As students are introduced to this purpose for composition, they need to be aware that there isn't just one right answer. They need to explore their own thinking and justify their own ideas. Fostering this creativity through critical thinking encourages students to think deeply about different topics and issues.

Common Ground for Composition Purposes

The purposes for composition outlined in this book are not all-encompassing, nor do they necessarily form an exhaustive list. A composition can take many forms and there can be many reasons for composing. However, the hope is that you will find most forms or motivations fit within these four overarching purposes. That being said, they are also certainly interrelated and have many common threads between them. Although I have written about each purpose separately in this chapter, it is important to note how the success criteria between the different purposes are very similar.

In fact, you will likely find that it can be difficult to create a composition prompt motivated purely for one of either reflection, entertainment, informative, or persuasion purposes, and that combining them can lead to a richer and more robust task. For example, students could compose (and perform!) a script that explains the benefits and dangers of using computers and other digital technologies, while also identifying protective responses. In many grades within the Health and Physical Education Curriculum, students are asked to consider the following questions: *What are some things you should do to use technology safely and in a way that supports your mental health? How can you get help if you get into trouble?* This example combines the purpose of entertaining with the purpose of informing in the composition and performance of a script as students inform their audience of the advantages and risks associated with using technology.

Compose to Reflect: Recall and Reflect

Recall What happened?	Big Idea:	
Reflect Describe the events sequentially.	First …	What feelings/emotions are connected to this event? Which senses can you use to help describe the event/experience fully? What did you see? What did you hear? What did you smell? What did you touch? What did you taste?
	Then …	
	Finally …	

Composing Prompt Cards: Recall and Reflect

RECALL AND REFLECT

Describe the time you were most proud of yourself.

RECALL AND REFLECT

Describe your favorite family vacation.

RECALL AND REFLECT

When did you learn a lesson you will never forget?

RECALL AND REFLECT

Describe a time when you were able to help someone.

RECALL AND REFLECT

What was your favorite trip ever?

RECALL AND REFLECT

Describe a time when you were brave.

Composing Prompt Cards: Recall and Reflect

RECALL AND REFLECT

Have you ever won something? Describe what you won and how you won it.

RECALL AND REFLECT

What was the best day of your life?

RECALL AND REFLECT

What was your favorite birthday like?

RECALL AND REFLECT

Describe a time when you learned something new about someone you love.

RECALL AND REFLECT

Describe a person in your life who has been influential. Why were/are they important? What did you learn from them?

RECALL AND REFLECT

Describe a time when you had to face one of your fears. What were you afraid of and how did you overcome it?

Compose to Entertain: A Story

Elements	Character(s)	Setting	Plot/Synopsis	Other
Questions to Consider	• How would I describe the main character? • What personality traits do they have? • How does this character change in my story? • Are there other characters I need to develop? • What supporting characters do I need?	• How would I describe the place where my story is set? • What is the time period? • What words could I use to describe the landscape? • What are the people of this place like?	• In what genre do I want to compose? • Why am I telling my story? • Are there challenges to overcome? Consequences of reactions by characters? • What motivations are needed? • Is there a "What if?" question I can use?	• Does my story have a theme or big idea I am trying to share? • Will the audience be comforted or challenged by my story? • What literary elements am I considering?
Thoughts				

Pembroke Publishers © 2025 *The New Literacy Block* by Lisa Donohue and Nicole Town ISBN 978-1-55138-376-7

Composing Prompt Cards: Entertaining Ideas

ENTERTAINING IDEAS

Imagine discovering a treasure from the past. What could you find, and what adventure could it take you on?

ENTERTAINING IDEAS

Imagine discovering a new species of plant or animal. Write about why your discovery is exciting and important.

ENTERTAINING IDEAS

Imagine waking up one morning to find out that your greatest wish has come true. What would your life be like?

ENTERTAINING IDEAS

Imagine discovering that you had magical powers. Write about the adventure this new discovery brings.

ENTERTAINING IDEAS

Imagine discovering a mythical creature. Write about the adventure you have with it.

ENTERTAINING IDEAS

Imagine discovering a time machine. Write about the adventure it takes you on.

Composing Prompt Cards: Entertaining Ideas

ENTERTAINING IDEAS

What would happen if you were taken on board an alien spaceship? Where would the aliens take you? What adventures would you have?

ENTERTAINING IDEAS

What would happen if you discovered an ancient key? What would it open? What adventure might it take you on?

ENTERTAINING IDEAS

What might happen if you were stranded on an island? Who would you be with? What might happen while you were there?

ENTERTAINING IDEAS

What might happen if you were invited to spend the night in an ancient castle? What secrets might you discover while you were there?

ENTERTAINING IDEAS

Have you ever had a day when everything seemed to go wrong? Write a humorous adventure about a character who has the worst luck. What kinds of things might go wrong for them? What lesson might this character learn in the end?

ENTERTAINING IDEAS

Write an adventure story about a character who comes face-to-face with their greatest fear. What might they be afraid of? How would the character overcome it?

Compose to Inform: Web Organizer

Use the following web to organize your information.

Supporting Details	Supporting Details

Big Idea	Big Idea

Topic

Big Idea	Big Idea

Supporting Details	Supporting Details

Composing Prompt Cards: Inform Me!

INFORM ME!

Are you an expert in something? What do you know a lot about? What else do you want to learn about it?

INFORM ME!

How could you teach someone to play your favorite sport or make your favorite food?

INFORM ME!

There are lots of powerful and important people in the world today. Who is someone you think has a lot of influence? Write about how and why this person became so important.

INFORM ME!

Many of the resources of the world are being reduced. In your opinion, what is the most important resource and how should it be protected?

INFORM ME!

Technology is evolving at a rapid pace. What is one thing that exists today that has revolutionized our world? Why is it so important?

INFORM ME!

What is a change happening in your community or city? How do you think it will affect the place where you live?

Compose to Persuade: Logic Table

Use the following table to organize your ideas.

State What is your Main Idea?	Topic	
Justify How can you prove it?	Big Idea	Supporting Evidence
	Big Idea	Supporting Evidence
	Big Idea	Supporting Evidence
Conclude What can you conclude?	Conclusion	

Composing Prompt Cards: HOT Topic

HOT TOPIC

Which animal would make the best class pet?

HOT TOPIC

If you met someone without any toys, which one of your toys would you share with them?

HOT TOPIC

Which is better: the pencil or the computer?

HOT TOPIC

If you could live anywhere in the world, where would you go?

HOT TOPIC

If you could meet anyone (dead or alive) who would you choose?

HOT TOPIC

If your pet could talk, what would you want to know?

Composing Prompt Cards: HOT Topic

HOT TOPIC

Who is the person who has had the most influence in your life?

HOT TOPIC

If you could travel to any event in history, what would you choose to witness first-hand?

HOT TOPIC

What would you do if you found something valuable that didn't belong to you?

HOT TOPIC

If you could take one modern invention into the past, what would you take and who would you share it with?

HOT TOPIC

What is something you never seem to have enough time for in your life?

HOT TOPIC

Do you feel that tests are the best way to measure your learning?

Composing Prompt Cards: HOT Topic

HOT TOPIC

If you were to create a time capsule, what would you put in it?

HOT TOPIC

If you could plan your next field trip, where would you like to go?

HOT TOPIC

How could you convince someone that it is important to respect the environment?

HOT TOPIC

What would you do if you discovered that your friend was being bullied?

HOT TOPIC

Imagine life in the future? What do you think will be the biggest change?

HOT TOPIC

If your school was given money to start a new program, what program would you like to see started?

Composing Prompt Cards: HOT Topic

HOT TOPIC

If you could be any character from a movie or a book, who would you like to be?

HOT TOPIC

If you could train a wild animal as a pet, which animal would you choose?

4 Purposeful Practice of Composition

As Purposeful Practice Time starts, the students all seem to go in different directions at once. Pausing to consult the tracking board, they gather the materials they require and set off to their designated tasks …

… **Scarlett** pauses, after examining the tracking board, to look at the piece of writing that her teacher modelled for the class. She reads it thoughtfully and then consults the chart with the success criteria. She makes one more stop at the interactive bulletin board, where she selects a familiar Entertaining Idea that she has been curious to expand on. She settles at her desk and begins to write. Pausing to reflect on the mentor text and the success criteria, Scarlett spends her time crafting her dialogue to develop her main character's relationship with the new species of animal they have discovered. She glances up and realizes that the first round of Purposeful Practice Time is almost over, so she takes a few moments to complete her thought. Just then, she hears the signal that indicates to the class that they should move on to their second task. Scarlett is invited to join her teacher at the conference table, so she gathers her work and is joined by a group of her fellow writers. They have all been diligently practicing using dialogue in their work to craft interesting characters. The teacher invites them to share with each other and provides them with an opportunity to give each other feedback. The teacher takes a moment or two to reflect on the compositions, ensuring that each student is able to express a personal goal. Scarlett writes hers on the top of her page so that she will be able to refer to it the next day as she continues to work on her writing. When the conference is over, Scarlett decides that she needs more time to think about what she would like to write next. With a few minutes remaining, she pulls out her independent reading book and settles down to read.

… **Ravi** grabs a classroom laptop computer and flips to his recording from the day before. After his composition conference, he decides that he needs more dialogue in order to add humour to engage his listeners. His peers gave him helpful suggestions, which he has now scribbled in the margins of his graphic organizer. Taking a deep breath, he begins to tackle the task of revising his work. He knows that he has solid ideas, and that he just needs his character to talk about the absurdity of his luck to really move the story along. Ravi begins to add to his graphic organizer to help organize his thinking. After a few minutes, he is ready to re-record some sections of his story. He adds dialogue where possible and, using his own style of editing, inserts or changes his work as necessary. When the teacher signals for everyone to move on to the second task, Ravi asks Liya if she could listen to his story and see if he has effectively added more dialogue. They head off to a quiet corner of the classroom and engage in a valuable peer conference. Ravi respects Liya's opinion and he's happy that she thinks he has made significant improvements to his work.

Likewise, Liya asks Danny for his opinion as she shares her writing with him. They are so engaged in their conversation that they don't realize when the teacher indicates that Purposeful Practice Time is over.

... **Miles** heads to his book box to grab his word-skills folder to get back to the task he was working on during transition time after recess. This week, the students are working on creating vocabulary cards for their new unit in Science. Miles has chosen the word *ecosystem* from the list the class generated in Science class and gets to work. He needs to define the word, use the word in a sentence, find out the number of syllables in the word, and identify the morphemes that make up the word. He turns to his friend Abby, who is also completing her own vocabulary card, and shows her the picture he has drawn for his word. She tells him to be sure to color it before he adds it to their Science Word Wall.

... Before beginning Purposeful Practice Time, **the teacher** has taken a few moments to review the daily tracking board to ensure that all students know which tasks they will be working on and in what order. She invites a few students to meet with her first so she can do a targeted decoding lesson. Once that has concluded, the teacher walks around the room to check in with students as they work on their various tasks. She noticed that Sophia has been slow to start the last couple times and pauses to touch base with her. After having a brief one-on-one conference, she gives the signal for the students to change to their second task.

The teacher now invites a couple of the students who have been working on their independent compositions to the conference table. Scarlett arrives along with three other students who have been focusing on using appropriate dialogue conventions in their writing. Some students have written a lot, and some have just started to edit their dialogue to include quotation marks. They take turns sharing their work and their ideas, and the teacher provides each student with immediate feedback. Each student writes at least one suggestion on the top of their page as a reminder of a specific writing goal to continue to work on in their writing. Scarlett has done some really good thinking and has started to apply her understanding of dialogue conventions to her own work. She plans to think more about how she could expand on the conversations in her story to make sure they are moving the plot along.

The conferences are over and the young writers head back to their desks. The teacher glances at the clock and notices that Purposeful Practice Time has come to an end. She signals for the class to finish up their tasks and to gather for Comprehension Time.

From Composition Time to Independent Composing

The key to successfully fitting all the components of Structured Literacy into the literacy block while still providing differentiated instruction and assessment opportunities for students begins in the first few days of school. Within these initial weeks, students can begin to develop solid routines that foster stamina and independence, giving the teacher time to provide small-group instruction and intervention targeted at and supportive of students' needs. At the beginning of the school year, introducing students to the crucial elements of the literacy block—whole-class direct instruction, collaborative and independent practice time—sets the foundation for a thriving learning environment. As you strategically teach students the different elements of the literacy block, it is possible to develop strong learning routines that continue to evolve and thrive throughout the school year.

Composition Time is perfect for explicit teaching of skills and strategies, followed by collaborative time to practice, and finally building stamina and independence through Purposeful Practice Time. By examining mentor texts, students can engage in rich dialogues and identify the elements that make each piece successful. Through these experiences and conversations, students become familiar with the skill targeted in the lesson, and then are able to apply this knowledge when composing independently, ensuring their time is well spent. They know what they need to be working on and have had an opportunity to see the skills in action. They have deconstructed mentor texts, examined student exemplars, or observed a writer's thinking in action. These whole-class activities provide the background knowledge that students can apply through their independent composition time, use as a basis for their feedback, and employ to set and monitor personal learning goals.

Composition Cycle

Students should have frequent ongoing opportunities to meet with the teacher and their peers for feedback. Often, a classroom full of writers is difficult to manage. It is hard to find time to conference with students individually or in small groups to monitor their learning—a real challenge when all students are composing simultaneously. If students are composing at different times through the literacy block, the teacher can strategically plan conferences to allow students immediate feedback on their work. In this manner, students can receive feedback on completed work or work in progress; this enables their learning to extend from one composition task to the next.

Imagine you have just finished a composition lesson at the beginning of your literacy block in the second or third week of school. You can think of learners in your class that would be ready to jump into their own compositions right away. At the same time, imagine another group of learners that needs more "think time." Some students may prefer to have this time to themselves, but we know that, for most students, purposeful classroom talk time can "provide necessary support to coherently bridge ideas and contributions, and to connect to an appropriate learning or teaching purpose" (Boyd & Markarian, 2015, p. 293). Providing these students time to share ideas and discuss their thinking with their peers *before* they begin the composition process can help them participate more effectively in independent Composition Time.

Fast-forward to the next day. These students are now ready to continue working on their compositions, having had an opportunity to conference with their peers and share their ideas, becoming more confident in their thinking. They relish more time to work on their composition, adding to their work as suggested or perhaps continuing to brainstorm ideas with increased vigor. Again, using independent composition time, they continue to build their skills. Finally, anxious to share, these students partner with peers again, recalling the conference from the previous day, to revisit personal goals and share ways in which they have applied them in their work.

SAMPLE COMPOSITION PURPOSEFUL PRACTICE TIME

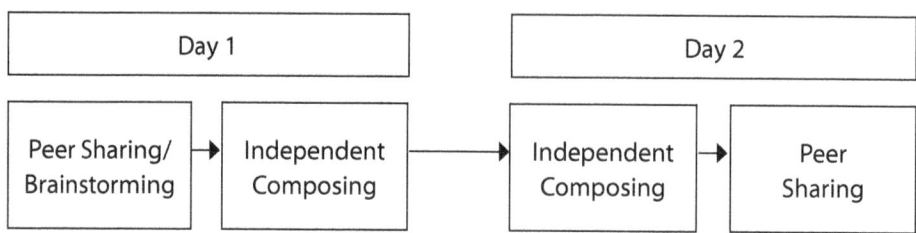

Again, through this simple sequence of tasks, students are able to talk through their ideas before independently working on their composition. They then receive immediate feedback to help them continue to improve their work. They use this independent composition time to practice and "try out" what they have been learning with the whole class during Composition Time. Regardless of the task, they have had an opportunity for explicit teaching and have worked with peers to construct their ideas confidently, becoming more familiar with what they need to try in order to be successful composers. They are now better prepared for a teacher conference, even if they don't have a completed piece of work; in fact, they can share and receive feedback on any piece at any stage in composition.

Why This Instructional Sequence Is So Powerful

Assessment and teaching go hand in hand. As you introduce students to new skills, you are constantly monitoring their learning through observations, conversations, and pieces of student work. You can use this ongoing assessment to provide students with feedback and assist them in setting new goals. Students need to be an active part of the assessment process, identifying their own strengths and setting personal learning goals. When you engage in frequent conversations with learners in small-group instruction and conferences, you can listen to students as they talk about their reading, writing, and thinking. You can gain insight into your students' strategies and processes and use it to provide them with immediate feedback and encouragement. In addition, removing the formal teacher conference from the cycle allows educators to be more flexible and meet with students for small-group instruction and conferences when needed and be responsive to the learners in front of them. When you use Purposeful Practice Time to provide focused small-group instruction in tandem with independent, scaffolded practice, you allow students to receive timely, relevant feedback. You are able to teach in a way that responds to individual learning needs and monitor progress as it pertains to each student's strengths and learning goals.

Constructing Purposeful Practice Time

To build strong literacy routines, students need to be able to work independently for sustained periods of time. Initially, this time could be as short as a few minutes, but it can gradually increase until students are able to work independently for approximately 15 to 20 minutes. That might not seem like a long time, but these minutes provide the framework upon which the entire literacy block will be built. It is essential that teachers take the time to lay the groundwork for these independent routines. Students need to understand the value of this independent time both to themselves and to their peers. Through independent time, students will practice and apply the skills they are learning throughout the remainder of the literacy block. They will consolidate their thinking and personalize their learning through the choices they make. Establishing the foundational independent routines is essential, as it provides opportunities for you to meet daily with small groups.

Have you ever engaged in a debate with a two-year-old? It is an argument you are certain to lose or at least surrender and walk away from. I remember many such conversations from when my children were younger. They would start innocently, with my making a statement, asking a question, or giving an instruction, only to be met with the charmingly innocent response, "… but *why*?" Drawn in by their charm and unaware of the direction the conversation was about to take, I would further explain my initial statement. This would lead to the now not-so-charming retort, "… but *why*?" The banter would continue for a while until, finally exasperated by the repeated "… but *why*?", I would firmly announce, "*Because it just is!*"—thus ending the conversation.

When it comes to establishing strong literacy routines, especially ones that require independence, "… but *why*?" is essential for youngsters to understand. They need to understand the purpose for their time and the value of the things they are going to be asked to do. They need to know that their work is valid, authentic, and important. They need to understand that it is not just that they are busying themselves so that the teacher can work with other kids, but rather that the work they are doing is helping them become better readers, writers, and learners. Their time is being well spent. Their work is important and they need to use their time wisely. When students understand the *why*, have sufficient choice in their work, and see the purpose for the tasks they are doing, they will likely be more engaged and focused, and better able to remain on task.

Building Stamina—Composition Routine

Imagine buying a new pair of running shoes, putting on a new pair of running shorts, and heading downtown to run your very first marathon on your first-ever day of running. Realistic? Of course not. In the same way, we wouldn't expect our students to return from a summer of playing outside (we'd like to think they also spent hours reading, but that's not very likely), flip open a book, and begin to read for a sustained period of time. Just as their muscles need to warm up for running, their brains need time to adjust to the demands of independent work time. For some students, the excitement of being in a classroom again with their best friend in the next desk and even the whirring noise of the fan are very real distractions from the texts they are trying to engage with. We need to help them build their stamina slowly, starting with short periods of time and gradually building on their successes until they are able to sustain their attention for 15 to 20 minutes.

Initially, students might be able to focus their attention and work independently for only a few minutes. It is better to start with a small goal and celebrate success with your students than to start with an unrealistic goal and face disappointment when they struggle or fail to reach it. You might say something like, "I know we've all been really busy all summer. Do you think we can all work independently for three minutes?" It might seem like a very short span of time and you may wonder why you should start with such a low target when clearly your students can work for a longer time. But it is better for them to meet with continued success and repeated praise than immediate frustration and possible disappointment. Track your students' accomplishments and increase the time they work independently every day. Each group of students is unique and the rate at which you increase the time will vary depending on their specific needs. If the time is increased in two-minute increments each day, within a few weeks students will have reached and exceeded the 15-minute goal.

What do you do with the student who decides to sharpen their pencil during independent practice time? What about the one who laughs out loud and just *needs* to share the funny part of their book with their neighbor? What do we do with someone who forgot their earphones for their audiobook, or the one who hasn't even started brainstorming ideas or using a graphic organizer to plan a single task? The burps, the giggles, the coughing fits—they all seem to happen right in the middle of independent work time. When routines are new, some students find it challenging to focus on the task at hand. The awkward silence can be strange for some youngsters, as they sit and wonder what others are reading, composing, thinking, or doing. For some, it is an odd feeling to be quiet together. For others, perhaps reading or thinking in their head is a skill they are still trying to master; you might see some youngsters mouthing words as they make sense of the words on the page.

Regardless of the challenges, it is important to remind students of the purpose of this valuable time. Some might benefit from spending one-on-one time with you, learning how to select books that are a good fit for them, books that they find interesting and can read successfully on their own. For the youngsters who need to share, building in a sharing time immediately following independent composition time allows them the opportunity to do just that. The first few days and weeks create the foundations on which the remainder of the literacy block will be built. If students are struggling with these initial routines, you might find it helpful to talk with them privately about the things they find challenging about this time. Allow them to get help from a friend when they are working to compose. Give them a quiet corner (or place on the carpet) where they can feel more comfortable or less awkward, or a place in the room where they can read aloud in a whisper in order to help them make sense of the texts they are reading. By setting realistic class goals, giving lots of positive reinforcement, and addressing specific needs of the learners, you can encourage all students to strive for independence.

In the same way that it would be impossible to run a marathon without proper shoes, students can't compose ideas for sustained periods of time without having something to think about. Prior to initiating the independent composing routine, consider the routines and spaces you will create for students to find inspiration. At the beginning of the school year, you might consider creating a classroom Box of Inspiration that contains images, headlines, prompts, thought-provoking questions, opinion statements, and anything else that might motivate students to compose. Perhaps students could bring in personal photographs of special places, people, pets, or events they wish to write about to add to their own composition inspiration page in a notebook. Consider creating a chart with the students about some things they might think about when planning a composition. At this early stage in the year, the focus for instruction is more on the routine of composing than on the content of what they create. By providing students with the structure of *when* and *why* to compose, we will later be able to invest the time in directly supporting them in improving *what* and *how* they write, speak, and create. Regardless of what they are working on, it is much harder for students to develop independent composition routines if we do not first help them find something to think about.

DAY ONE

(Instructional time: approximately 25 minutes)
Begin by gathering the students together as a large group.

> *Today, we are going to add another important element to our independent work routines. We will begin our independent composition time. Take a moment to think: Why is writing and creating important?*

Allow students a few moments to think about this question and share their thoughts with a partner. Select a few students to share their thinking with the class. As they share, record their thinking on a chart to keep for later reference.

> *There are many reasons why writing is important. We can use writing to share our ideas with others or to help us organize our own thinking. Sometimes we write things down so we don't forget something important. Other times we might write so that someone else can learn how to do something new. We might write a story to entertain our friends or a letter to share news with a friend, or we could write a list of things we need to buy at the grocery store. We use writing in lots of different ways and they are all very important.*
>
> *Now, think about some things that you can do to become a better writer.*

Again, allow students an opportunity to share their ideas with their partners and then with the larger group. Continue to add their ideas to the chart.

> *We can all become better writers by practicing our writing, trying to write for different purposes, and sharing our writing with others. Sometimes when our friends read our writing, they can give us some ideas that can help us to become better writers. We can learn to use more interesting words and more description so that the people who read our writing can imagine in their own minds the things we write about.*
>
> *Finally, think about everyone in our class writing independently. What would that look like? What would it sound like?*

After students share their thinking with their partners, again record their thinking on the chart.

SAMPLE CHART: COMPOSITION INDEPENDENT PRACTICE

Why is writing/creating important?	What would it look like?
• We can share our ideas with others. • We can write down things that we want to remember. • It can help us organize our ideas. • We can reflect on our thinking. • We can entertain/inform/persuade others.	• Everyone would be working at their desk or in a quiet spot. • Everyone would stay in the spot they chose. • We would be writing/creating the whole time. • Sometimes we might need to pause and think.

How can we learn to be better writers?	What would it sound like?
• We can learn how to encode words. • We can learn to use better words. • We can compose for different purposes and audiences. • We can share our thinking with our friends and ask for feedback. • We can set goals for ourselves and work towards them. • We can use a dictionary or thesaurus to check/fix our work.	• It would be really quiet. • We would all be thinking and composing on our own.

Do you remember when we said that our brains were a little like our muscles and they need exercise in order to work for longer periods of time? Well, today we are going to start exercising our "composing muscles." We are going to work independently for five minutes. We will all have an opportunity to share our thinking with a friend once the time is over. Before we get started, take a minute to think about a topic you'd like to write or create something about.

If the class has already created a list of potential topics, this would be a good time to revisit it or to encourage students to look through the inspiration images and ideas they have collected. Start as soon as the students all seem ready to begin and have found a suitable place (and have their pencils sharpened).

We are going to work for five minutes starting now.

While students are working, resist the urge to wander around the classroom. Choose a spot where you can observe the students without standing directly over them. Again, the best option would be to sit at the table you plan to use for small-group instruction. That way, the students become familiar with the routine of working independently while you are working elsewhere in the room.

At the end of five minutes, gently indicate to students that the composition time is now over and they need to come back together as a class.

Creators! You have had an opportunity to work independently for five minutes. When we compose, it's nice to share our work with our peers. Let's all find a partner and share our work with them.

Encourage students to partner up and share their composition with a classmate. Students might need guidance in responding in positive ways and saying only supportive things to each other (constructive feedback, and no criticism or put-downs allowed).

How did you feel about composing for five minutes? Do you think you can work for a little bit longer next time? Tomorrow, our goal will be to practice composing independently for seven minutes. For now, please put your work away so you will have it when you need it again.

Congratulations! It may not seem like a significant moment, but you have begun to lay the essential building blocks for a complete literacy block. When you invest time in establishing routines for independent practice time, students will understand that the work they do independently is just as important as the work they do directly with the teacher. Independent work is not busy-work! It is an important time that students can use to work toward their individual learning goals.

DAY TWO AND BEYOND

On the second day of building the independent routines, begin by reviewing the charts you constructed with the students. You might ask if they would like to make any additions or changes. If you help them understand the purpose of their independent work, students will see it as important, meaningful, and authentic. Students might wish to share some of the things they enjoyed or discovered during their independent work time. For example, some students might want to share something interesting that they created during their composing time or an idea that they were excited to continue writing about.

Over the next week, repeat the procedure, taking a few minutes each day to review the charts, answer questions, and address any challenges that students might be facing. Gradually increase the time students spend working independently until they are able to complete independent composing for the desired length of time. This target will vary according to the age of the students and their individual needs, but 15 to 20 minutes is a reasonable goal.

As students become more comfortable with the routine of working independently, they need to understand that during this time you will be working with other students. At first, the students might find this distracting; they might pause while working to observe or listen to the conversation you are having with other students. Over time, students will learn that everyone's work is important, both the work they are doing independently and the work that others might be doing with the teacher.

Keys to Success: Independent Composing Time
- Students are able to self-select topics or use a class inspiration guide for support with composition.
- Students are able to select an appropriate area where they can work independently.
- Students understand the purpose and value of composing independently.
- Stamina is built until students can work independently for 15–20 minutes.
- Students are able to independently solve problems that might arise, such as spell unfamiliar words (encoding) without asking or ignore distractions.
- Students can access resources, if necessary, such as a dictionary or thesaurus.
- A washroom procedure is established that allows students to go when necessary without needing to ask the teacher, such as signing out or putting a washroom pylon on their desk.
- Students have opportunities to share periodically.

Scholars! You have all been working hard to build up your stamina when working independently. Today while you are working, I am going to ask a few people to work with me at our conference table. We will use whisper-voices so that we don't disturb you. You need to keep doing your work because we all have very important jobs to do. I promise that everyone will have a chance to work with me at the conference table. But when it is not your turn, you need to be working on your own important thinking.

You might wish to use this initial time to gather assessment data and begin to assess students' individual strengths and needs. Encoding (spelling) is an important skill that you may wish to complete an assessment for to support your planning and creation of small groups for instruction. Many assessments are commonly used to identify students who are struggling with spelling and to pinpoint specific areas of difficulty with phonological encoding. Alternatively, you may wish to conference with individual students to chat about their interests or feelings toward writing and other composition tasks in order to gather information to inform your planning and instruction of composition throughout the year. No matter how you choose to use this time, it will be important to continue to reinforce the importance of the work students are doing, both independently and at the conference table with you. Once you have completed your initial assessments and the students have had sufficient time to develop the routines of independence, you are ready to start using this time to conduct small-group interventions and instruction.

As students become more comfortable with this routine, a visual tracking board might help them stay organized, such as the one described in Chapter 2. This visual reminder will make it easier for students to see which literacy elements they are working on and when. On a tracking board, this might look a little like the following:

SAMPLE TRACKING BOARD: COMPOSITION PURPOSEFUL PRACTICE, DAY 1

Group	First I will ...	Then I will ...
Group 1	Peer Sharing/Brainstorming	Independent Composing

SAMPLE TRACKING BOARD: COMPOSITION PURPOSEFUL PRACTICE, DAY 2

Group	First I will ...	Then I will ...
Group 1	Independent Composing	Peer Sharing

Embedding Foundational Language Skills

As students begin to engage in authentic composition and comprehension situations, it becomes possible for the teacher to monitor their understanding of competence in the building blocks of communication. Throughout instructional time, teacher and students can engage in conversations about decoding and encoding multisyllabic words (including phonemic awareness), morphological knowledge, frequent word usage, syntax and grammar, or transcription skills to determine which words or word skills need to be a focus for continued learning. For example, a teacher observes that one student is unsure how to write verbs in the past tense (for example, regular verbs: *walked*, *played*; irregular verbs: *ran* instead of *runned*, *ate* instead of *eated*), another student has frequent substitutions due to word-usage errors (for example, *there/their/they're*), and another needs to strengthen their repertoire of frequently used words (*because*, *said*, *went*, etc.).

These skills should also be embedded into the literacy block routines to allow students multiple opportunities to practice working with words. You can provide daily practice time during Transition Activities, as well as build it into your Purposeful Practice Time to offer sufficient opportunity throughout a weekly cycle for students to engage in word skills. Several skills would be best supported through explicit and systematic instruction, including phonics, orthographic and morphological knowledge, vocabulary, syntax and sentence structure, grammar, and capitalization and punctuation. By providing focused time for understanding and manipulating words, you support students' development of skills from both Scarborough's Reading Rope and Sedita's Writing Rope.

Transition Activities and Word Skills Cycle

While many teachers have moved away from traditional spelling textbooks and weekly spelling lists, word skills remain an important aspect of regular literacy instruction. The hot debate about whether to teach spelling has resulted in many teachers being unsure about how to effectively develop proficiency with this skill. Weekly spelling lists don't provide the differentiation and personalization necessary for students to transfer their learning to their writing, but there remains a need to actively teach word skills, word meanings, and various word patterns.

Embedding a decoding and encoding routine into authentic vocabulary instruction can provide opportunities for students to work with words in a meaningful way, as they will be more likely to transfer their use of morphology and spelling patterns in new writing situations. As we unpack the Science of Reading, many teachers have become aware of terminology such as *orthographic mapping*, *decoding*, *encoding*, *morphology*, and *vocabulary*. However, the question remains for many of us: *What does it all mean?*

Vocabulary is the body of words a person knows, understands, and can use in various contexts, such as listening, speaking, reading, and writing. A person's vocabulary is key to their comprehension of texts and ability to communicate clearly and precisely with others. Consequently, vocabulary instruction is paramount to providing instruction not only in reading and writing, but also in content. When we widen a child's knowledge of words, we widen their worlds, enabling them to grasp content, connect ideas, and communicate more effectively. This is probably why Vaughn *et al.* (2022) recommend "explicitly build[ing] students' world and word knowledge … [by] build[ing] different aspects of word knowledge and skills so that students can determine the meanings of words" (p. 22).

"A word is a small magic, a spell that can unlock the world." —Jane Yolen

Given what we know about how people develop language skills, students build their vocabulary and apply it to written language through the process of orthographic mapping. According to Susan Smartt and Deb Glaser in their book *Next Steps in Literacy Instruction*, orthographic mapping refers to the automatic word recognition that results from neural pathways created in the brain that link sound (phonemes) to written symbols (graphemes) so we can decode and create meaning. *Decoding* is another word for the reading process used to peel words off the page—the brain translates written words into spoken words in order to read. The process also supports encoding as we think about converting spoken language into print—spelling! Encoding is the segmenting of the sounds we hear in a word in order to represent each sound and write them using the appropriate spelling. This is when many teachers might be asking themselves: *Are my students able to decode letter sounds and blend them together to say a word?* Or, *Are my students able to segment and isolate the sounds in spoken words to spell them in print?*

Encoding is considered a much more complex skill than decoding as it involves more aspects of word memory. Researchers have found that *most* spelling can be explained by word memory processes, such as sound structure (phonology), meaningful parts (morphemes/morphology) and a word's role in the sentence formation (syntax) (Moats, 2019). Good spellers have a better understanding of all the processes, while those who struggle with spelling often have incomplete or inaccurate understanding of one or more word memory processes. According to Moats (2019), "reading words is easier than spelling them because words can be recognized on the basis of partial or degraded word memories, whereas spelling requires complete and accurate word memories" (p. 17). This explains why some students are strong, fluent readers, yet wrestle with spelling words they can easily read.

Effective instruction in both decoding and encoding is crucial for all students, as these skills serve as building blocks for more advanced literacy skills like reading comprehension and writing composition. Explicit and systematic instruction within a structured literacy block is vital for student success. The English language system has a clear structure, and students need to understand the patterns in language to help them read and write efficiently.

Although this book will not get into the specifics of this instruction, a general outline of where to begin and how to build students' knowledge for word reading and spelling is outlined below (from Moats, 2019):

- Beginning to Spell: Phoneme Awareness, Letter Sounds, and Letter Names
- Learning Phoneme-Grapheme Correspondences
- Words with Less Predictable or Odd Spellings
- Orthographic Patterns and Position Constraints
- Inflections and Suffix Change Rules
- Multi-syllable Words and Schwa
- Latin-based Prefixes, Suffixes, and Roots

Teachers will want to determine the level of students' word-solving skills (using assessment for learning) so they know where to pick up instruction or provide targeted interventions (Vaughn *et al.*, 2022). In general, by the junior or intermediate grades, teachers will be working on multisyllabic word-solving strategies and morphology with the majority of students in a class. Vaughn *et al.* (2022) propose choosing a routine to develop students' ability to decode multisyllabic words. "Rather than teaching a wide array of rules, choose a routine that provides simple steps for breaking words into parts and blending those parts together to sound out the word" (Vaughn *et al.*, 2022, p. 6). The routine I often choose (from Vaughn *et al.*, 2022, p. 7) to work through with students not only focuses on using phonics knowledge (vowel teams to identify syllables) but also builds students' morphological knowledge. Morphology is the study of how morphemes (the smallest units of language that have meaning) are used to form words.

Building this knowledge helps students to keep in mind that the words they read and write have meaning on their own as well as in context with other words. Remember that each class and community is different and you should always select routines and instructional strategies that will work best for the students in front of you.

DAY ONE

(Instructional time: approximately 25 minutes)
Begin by gathering the students in a large group.

Today, we are going to add another really important element to our independent work routines. We are going to begin our study of word skills. Take a moment to think to yourself: Why is it important to know how words are formed?

Allow students a few moments to think about this question and share with a partner. Select a few students to share their thinking with the class. As they share, record their thinking on a chart to keep for later reference.

There are many reasons why working with words is important. We can use word skills to read unfamiliar words. Sometimes when we write things down, word skills help us to spell words correctly so we can communicate clearly. We might want to use new words in our writing that we've never had to spell before. Word skills can help us solve for words we don't know yet. We use words in lots of different ways, and they are all very important.

Now think about some things you can do to become a better reader and speller.

Again, allow students an opportunity to share their ideas with their partners and then with the large group. Continue to add their ideas to the chart.

We can all become better readers and writers by practicing our word skills, learning about word patterns, and sharing how we use morphemes to help us communicate. Sometimes when we work with words, getting support and ideas from friends helps us understand words better. We can learn to use more interesting words and more syllable knowledge when reading and writing so that we can become more efficient.

Finally, think about everyone working on word skills in our class. What would that look like? What would it sound like?

After students share their thinking with their partners, again record their thinking on the chart.

SAMPLE CHART: WORD SKILLS PURPOSEFUL PRACTICE

Why is working with words important?	What would it look like?
• We can read unfamiliar words. • We can spell new words. • It can help us become more automatic in reading and writing (spelling). • It can help us develop our vocabulary. • It can help us understand and use new words in other subjects.	• Everyone would be working at their desk or in a quiet spot. • Everyone stays in the spot they chose. • We would be working with words the whole time. • Sometimes we might need to pause and think. • Sometimes we might ask a friend for help.
How can we learn to be better readers and spellers?	What would it sound like?
• We can learn how to decode unfamiliar words more automatically. • We can build our vocabulary using morphological knowledge to comprehend new words. • We can learn how to encode (spell) new words more accurately. • We can focus on organizing our thoughts rather than getting stuck with spelling. • We can share our thinking with our friends and ask for feedback.	• It would be quiet. • We would all be thinking. • If we ask a friend for help, we use a whisper voice so we don't disturb others.

Do you remember when we talked about morphemes? Morphemes are the smallest units of language that have meaning. Today, we are going to learn a routine for breaking longer words into parts so we can easily sound them out. Please pull out your word-skills notebooks so you can complete the activity along with me. (Pause for students to get out their materials.)

Purposeful Practice of Composition

There are four steps in this routine. In step 1, we circle the prefixes and suffixes in the word. The first word is unreasonable. *I am going to circle* un- *because it is a prefix and* -able *because it is a suffix. Remember* un- *means* not *and* -able *means* capable of being.

The teacher refers to the routine posted in the classroom on chart paper for future reference. This routine could also be printed and glued into notebooks for students to use when they are completing various word-skills activities. As the teacher refers to each step, she explicitly models it for students on the board where everyone can clearly see.

In step 2, I am going to underline the vowel sounds that are left. I am going to underline ea *and* o. *I am doing this because each syllable has a vowel sound.* (Pause for students to complete in their notebook.)

In step 3, I am going to use my pencil to loop under each word part as I say it: un rea son able. (Pause again.)

Now, in step 4, I am going to blend the parts together: unreasonable. Unreasonable *means* not capable of reason or explanation.

The teacher follows the same procedure for two more multisyllabic word examples of their choice. It is best to select words that are authentic to the learning of the class. They may be examples of vocabulary that students are learning in a different subject, or that the class has come across in a recent read-aloud.

At the end of the lesson, the teacher reviews the routine before asking the students to try applying the routine themselves.

Language Architects! You have had an opportunity to follow me. When we work on word skills during Purposeful Practice Time, it's nice to share our work with our peers. Let's all find a partner and try the list of words on the board together.

Encourage students to partner up and complete a list of five to seven words together. Again, the words may be examples of vocabulary that students are learning in a different subject, or that the class has come across in a recent read-aloud. Another option is to engage in a word-skills game or activity with the class to encourage them to apply the routine you have just worked on.

How did you feel about working with words today? Do you think that we can add this kind of work to our Purposeful Practice Time? Tomorrow, our goal will be to practice another activity that you may have the choice of working on during word-skills time. For now, please put your work away so you will have it when you need it again.

You might choose to include this instruction during a Composition Time in your initial building of your literacy block. On the other hand, you might also consider building this into your literacy block cycle by initiating a routine like "Morphology Mondays!" and doing a lesson weekly.

The "Word Skills Task Cards" on page 82 can help students explore words and word patterns through authentic reading experiences. Readers generate word meanings and integrate them into existing vocabulary through repeated exposure in meaningful contexts. The tasks are designed to strengthen students' vocabulary and word skills. Some tasks are intended to encourage students to attend to new and interesting vocabulary, some introduce students to various parts of speech, and others help students develop an understanding of new words through a morphological approach. Students encounter new words in all text forms, so these tasks are easily used for both fiction and nonfiction texts.

Transcription Practice

Printing, Handwriting, and Word Processing

Although there was a period of time when printing, handwriting, and word processing were removed from many curricula, research has shown that "early handwriting instruction improves students' writing. Not just its legibility, but its quantity and quality" (Graham, 2009–2010, p. 20). For many students, the skill to print or handwrite can place constraints on writing progress if not effectively developed. Teachers need to cultivate printing, handwriting, and word processing skills in order to allow students to develop the ability to translate the ideas in their minds into written text at a reasonable rate.

Embedding a routine for these skills into Purposeful Practice Time can provide opportunities for students to develop fluent, legible handwriting. In this way, students will more likely be able to focus on the many other skills of writing (such as generating and organizing ideas, making word choices to establish voice, developing syntactic awareness) in composition (specifically writing) opportunities.

Again, a tracking board might help students to stay organized. This visual reminder will make it easier for students to see which literacy elements they are working on, and when. The tracking board might look a little like this:

SAMPLE TRACKING BOARD: COMPOSITION PURPOSEFUL PRACTICE, DAY 1

Group	First I will …	Then I will …
Group 1	**Words Skills**	**Transcription Practice**

As each student is unique, so too is each class. Only you can decide, using your best judgment, when the time is right to introduce your students to the various independent purposeful practice elements of the daily literacy block. In some cases, you might choose to introduce students to words skills practice simultaneously with independent composing and independent reading, as they all require a similar set of routines and behavioral expectations. Or it might be better to introduce the word-skills routine once students have had a few days to develop independent composing and reading routines. Either way, the principles of each are very similar: to foster independence, you must let students understand the purpose of their work and have the opportunity to gradually increase their stamina when working.

Purposeful Practice of Composition

Word Skills Task Cards

WORD SKILLS

Morpheme Hunt

Become a morpheme collector by hunting for all the words in a passage of your text that use the following suffixes. Keep a record of your words in the chart to see how many you can find!

-ed	-ly	-ful

WORD SKILLS

Word Sums

Find five words and create word sums to show how the words are built.

Example: re + build + ing = rebuilding

WORD SKILLS

Glossary

Create a glossary of new vocabulary that you've learned while engaging with a passage in your text. Beside each word, write its meaning. You might need to check in a dictionary or with another source to verify that you're sure what the word means.

WORD SKILLS

Word Choice

Find a passage from the text that shows how the author used their choice of words to help share the message. It might be a very descriptive part of a story or a very informative section of a nonfiction resource. Which **Tier 2** vocabulary (words) were the most powerful to you as the reader?

5 Comprehension: Reading, Listening, Viewing

The recess bell rings and the students enter the classroom to begin their bell work. After everyone has settled in and had some time to quietly work on some word-skills exercises, the teacher draws their attention to the magnetic board showing talk-partners and they quickly scan the chart for their names and move to sit with their partners. Brooke is excited because Dylan is her partner; Quinn quietly sits beside Omar, who waves shyly; Anna whispers something in Russian to Kristina and both girls begin to giggle.

The teacher begins by setting the context for the book. She shares that the author is Nandini Ahuja and the illustrator is Anoosha Syed. Both women are of South Asian background (Indian and Pakistani) and now live in the United States. Nandini Ahuja lives in New York with her husband and works as a social worker. Anoosha Syed is a Pakistani-Canadian illustrator and lives in Dallas, Texas. Her students know that accurately identifying who is telling the story and where they are from is a way of showing respect, one of the principles of Indigenous Storywork. She then asks the students to recall a time when they recognized a need to advocate for something in order to prompt them to think about the background knowledge they might use to engage with this text. They share their ideas with their talk-partners, recalling the reasons they were passionate about making a change and the ways in which students asked others to help them. After a few brief moments, the teacher introduces some of the vocabulary and background knowledge students will need in order to engage with the text being read today. She has written some of the words and adds any talking points on a chart so that students can refer back to the funds of knowledge for the duration of the read-aloud. Today, the teacher also highlights a question for the students to consider: "Farah is very passionate about making a change in her community. Is there a cause you feel passionate about that would make our world a better place?" After she reads the question, she allows the students a moment to think about what the question is asking and paraphrases as needed.

The teacher reads the book *Rise Up and Write It*, written by Nandini Ahuja and illustrated by Anoosha Syed. Throughout the reading, she pauses a few times to think aloud or define an unfamiliar term. While reading, she poses a few questions and asks the students to talk to their partners. They all turn and talk, taking a minute or so to verbalize their ideas. The teacher is cautious to balance the need to pause, think, and talk with maintaining the flow of the book. She knows that pausing too frequently, or talking for too long, can interrupt the content of the book and distract students from the main message.

After she has finished reading the book, the teacher draws the student's attention back to the question she posed before reading. Brooke and Dylan get into a passionate dialogue; the teacher can hear them strongly stating their ideas and referring to the book to justify their answers. Quinn and Omar sit in silence for a few seconds and then Omar begins to whisper his thoughts to his partner. Anna and Kristina begin to talk, but the conversation quickly switches from English to Russian, as Kristina discovers that she can't find the exact words to express herself in English, her new language. The teacher listens in on the various conversations, allowing sufficient time for students to fully explain their thinking.

Using a signal, the teacher indicates that the students should finish their conversations. They end by thanking their partners and turn their attention back to the whole class. The teacher again restates the question. Almost every hand is raised to respond. Brooke and Dylan are practically crawling over each other, eager to share their discussion with the class. Omar raises a cautious hand and, when the teacher calls on him, shares his thinking with a rather coy smile. Perhaps there is time for one or two more responses. When students share simple answers, the teacher probes deeper into their thinking by asking, "What made you think that?" or "How do you know?" Finally, Anna is asked to share. She pauses and casts a sideways glance at Kristina, who bursts into a fit of giggles once again. Anna shares Kristina's thinking, explaining that her ideas were really interesting because the story made her think of a time she had in her home country. The conversations are rich and alive. The students' ideas are profound and relevant. In this short time, the students have actively connected with a book, engaged in rich conversations, and practiced higher-order thinking.

Reading Comprehension as an Outcome

For so many of us, reading instruction has often been centred around reading strategies and metacognition to build comprehension, the goal of reading. In the past, much of the work surrounding reading comprehension has focused on explicitly teaching students strategies such as connecting, inferring, questioning, visualizing, determining importance, and synthesizing. These strategies helped form our understanding as educators of what effective reading-comprehension instruction was supposed to look like in our classrooms.

While comprehension strategies will still form an essential part of the toolkit students use to build comprehension and understand text, these are not the only skills students need to be able to read. It is therefore vital for educators to begin with a summary of how the brain learns to read and the strategies and steps that support this process for students.

This is essential for a few reasons, three of which I have outlined here. First, written language (and therefore reading) is a human invention. Thus, learning to read is not a natural process as no part of the brain is designed for reading; we must train other parts of the brain to take up this function. This is important to acknowledge as it highlights the need for educators to engage in explicit and systematic instruction when they teach students how to read. Second, reading comprehension is not a singular skill developed through a variety of strategies; rather, it is an outcome of many skills and strategies that come together to shape skilled readers. Third, and finally, there is no program, curriculum, or text that teaches students; teachers do. Consequently, building our understanding of how the brain learns to read will support and empower educators to use their professional judgment to make decisions and plan for the implementation of curriculum in a way that will enable students to learn.

As you familiarize yourself with what neuroscience tells us about how students learn to read in this chapter and beyond, remembering that skilled reading is an outcome will make the planning, instruction and assessment of comprehension more accessible.

The Neuroscience of Learning to Read

The Science of Reading is a body of research and evidence that helps us understand how students learn to read. We can start with the Simple View of Reading (SVR) presented by Gough and Tunmer in 1986. The SVR is a formula demonstrating that reading has two basic components: word recognition (decoding) and language comprehension as shown below:

$$\text{Decoding (D)} \times \text{Language Comprehension (LC)} = \text{Reading Comprehension (RC)}$$

This formulaic presentation of reading comprehension as an outcome of multiplying decoding skills and language comprehension skills demonstrates that students must have both sets of skills to be able to read with understanding and comprehend written texts.

As Farrell, Hunter, Davidson, and Osenga explain:

> Gough and Tunmer (1986) proposed the Simple View of Reading to clarify the role of decoding in reading. Many educators did and still do believe that strong decoding skills are not necessary to achieve reading comprehension if language abilities are strong. Beginning and struggling readers are often taught to compensate for weak decoding by guessing an unfamiliar word based on the first letter or the picture, then asking themselves if the word makes sense after reading the sentence. In contrast, when decoding is the focus of instruction students are taught to sound out unfamiliar words using all the letters and to practice reading accurately until an adequate reading rate is achieved, along with accurate decoding (n.d., para. 4).

Following the work of Gough and Tunmer, Scarborough's Reading Rope emerged in the early 1990s to expand on the SVR. Hollis Scarborough developed the Reading Rope model to show the micro skills that make up the intricacies of word recognition (decoding) and language comprehension. According to the article "Can Scarborough's Reading Rope Transform the Approach to Literacy Instruction?" (n.d.), in the early rendition of the original model, Scarborough used pipe cleaners to show how the different "strands" of reading are woven together yet independent of one another. She used this visual to demonstrate for parents the skills their children needed to develop into skilled readers.

On the word recognition (decoding) side of the rope, the strands include the skills of phonological awareness, decoding—consisting of alphabetic principle and letter-sound correspondences—and sight recognition, including fluency. On the language comprehension side of the rope, the strands include background knowledge, vocabulary, language structures, verbal reasoning, and literacy knowledge. This model is particularly helpful from an intervention perspective as it can help educators direct targeted support to the specific component(s) of reading that a student might be struggling to develop. Before we can support comprehension of written text, we need to ensure that both parts of the rope are intact and being woven together in an increasingly strategic and automatic manner, further demonstrating why we cannot just teach reading strategies.

THE SCIENCE OF READING IS NOT JUST FOR THE PRIMARY GRADES!

The Science of Reading is continuing to gain traction, and the foundational work is being incorporated into primary literacy classrooms everywhere. However, although we know that early intervention is best, no matter what grade is being taught, we are working with students who have gaps in their instruction across the various strands of the rope.

It is our collective responsibility as educators to "catch-up" students or close gaps in reading in order to provide equal access to the education all students have a fundamental human right to. The Ontario Human Rights Commission (2024) found that "no other skill taught in school and learned by school children is more important than reading. It is the gateway to all other knowledge. If children do not learn to read efficiently, the path is blocked to every subject they encounter in their school years" (The consequences of not teaching children to read section, para. 9). This is especially apparent when we consider literacy instruction beyond the primary level. This is where we can see educators transitioning their instruction from a learning-to-read approach to a reading-to-learn process that is pervasive across subjects and disciplines.

Intervention for struggling readers is effective only when it targets students' specific areas of need (Farrell, Hunter, Davidson, and Osenga, n.d.). Therefore, as educators consider the Reading Rope model, we can use it to help us make research-based decisions to support students with greater intentionality. As mentioned in chapter 2, educators can use universal screening assessment data to identify students who need intervention and can collect further data related to specific strands of the Reading Rope to inform instruction. According to Ontario Human Rights Commission (2024, Early Screening section), universal screening involves conducting standardized screening assessments on every student. These common assessments are completed with students using evidence-based tools that have established reliability and validity standards that ensure confidence in their effectiveness. They can be used to facilitate interventions, while reducing the potential for bias since schools can compare results from common screening tools across various populations.

Farrell, Hunter, Davidson, and Osenga (n.d.) also point out that it is important that scores from assessments provide enough information for educators to determine specific decoding or language comprehension skills that need targeted instruction. These scores can then be used to inform instruction in whole-class and small groupings, depending on the variety of needs present in the class. It will also be vital for educators to engage in ongoing monitoring of progress to ensure that the interventions and targeted instruction are in fact improving students' abilities. This aligns with the purpose of screening and data collection, which is to ensure students and teachers have the resources they need to succeed.

Comprehension and the Literacy Block

If I'm no longer building my Comprehension Time around reading comprehension strategies, what am I doing? Just as we have used the Science of Reading to identify the specific components of reading a student might be struggling with, we can also use the Reading Rope framework to help us build the essential components of skilled reading in a structured way. By addressing each strand, we support students' development into skilled readers who not only decode words but also fully understand and engage with the text. Although it will vary depending on the specific instructional needs of each class, when we move beyond the primary grades much of this whole-class instructional time will be spent on building skills from the language comprehension side of the rope.

The comprehension strands of the rope incorporate many of the facets of receptive language. This comes with the understanding that we need to be building language comprehension skills since reading comprehension is an outcome of skilled reading. Given this understanding, we can think about how we are providing instruction around language comprehension strategies through a variety of texts since students can demonstrate these skills after reading, viewing, or listening to a text. In Chapter 2, I shared that this time could be used to engage in lessons focused on modelling fluency, using think-aloud strategies to explicitly introduce various thinking moves, or posing critical-thinking questions and encouraging students to talk with each other about various texts. All of this (and more!) can be efficiently and effectively achieved through reading aloud to students.

> "In reading aloud, an effective teacher serves as an orchestra conductor, coordinating conversation among students, fostering aesthetic and efferent text responses, pushing students' text reaction past surface-level responses, and weaving an intricate network of meaning." (International Literacy Association, 2018)

Working with Stories in a Meaningful Way

When preparing a read-aloud for my class, I am often reminded of all the times I was read to as a child. My childhood was full of stories—library trips to gather books, movies of fairytales and adventures full of drama, audiobooks on long car rides, listening to my family recall countless stories at regular gatherings, and bedrooms with bookshelves for the books we annually received as presents from my Grandma Town. My mother had a particularly interesting habit of reading aloud to us while we were sitting at the dinner table; she said it was because my siblings and I took forever to eat and she would have died of boredom otherwise!

I think the most important realization I have had from these experiences is that many of my interactions with stories were just that—I engaged with the text for no other reason than to listen to, read, or watch them, oftentimes over and over again because I loved them so much. Certainly, I enjoyed the vibrant conversations that regularly happened with my family about what we were reading. However, there were no reading responses to write or themes or big ideas I was tasked with determining; I just engaged with stories for personal reflection and enjoyment. I believe this is a big part of the reason why I *love* stories.

When learning about Storywork through Jo-Ann Archibald's book *Indigenous Storywork* (2008), I really connected with the notion that "stories have their own life … because sometimes when you tell a story to a hunter, the hunter will take, interpret that story differently than say the basket maker. And the basket maker may remember other details. So the story takes on a life of its own and travels from person to person" (p. 97). Throughout her work, Archibald identifies Storywork as having seven principles that provide a framework for engaging with stories. As I work with stories using that framework, the story becomes the teacher and I can help to facilitate each individual students' learning by considering what ideas will help me get started on the pathway to working with stories in meaningful ways.

In my classroom practice, I now make a promise to read aloud to my students every day. I am always awed by the intensity with which so many of them listen while I read. While yes, we do often engage in deep and thoughtful conversations, we sometimes simply "read" so everyone can take what they need from the text.

So give yourself grace, and remember, it's OK sometimes to just read.

Read-Alouds

Teacher-led read-alouds play a critical role in helping children acquire and develop the foundational skills and knowledge they need to become readers. Read-alouds during Comprehension Time allow opportunities for teachers to model engagement with texts. Students can see what good readers do when they read. When we read aloud, we provide students with the opportunity to learn a great deal about reading and the comprehension process. We are able to explicitly teach comprehension and thinking strategies, promote higher-order thinking, and encourage rich conversations about texts. We are also able to teach things implicitly—things like passion for reading, reading with excitement or anticipation, and getting humor or pure enjoyment from texts. We can help foster curiosity, we can build vocabulary, we can extend beyond texts by continuing the conversation or exploring new ideas. Through intentional teacher-student-book interactions, we demystify the thinking processes that happen when we read. We can think out loud for students to gain an understanding of the invisible thought processes. Reading aloud is the time when we help students see the value of reading, understand the purpose of reading, and develop a passion for reading.

Read-alouds are the vehicle through which we are able to directly teach the whole class and develop shared understanding around specific learning goals. This instructional time is far more than time spent entertaining children by reading a book to them. It has significant value.

This process of reading and thinking aloud with students is an integral component of teaching comprehension, as supported by decades of research. The International Literacy Association (2018) points out that "there is a direct causal relationship between reading to children at a young age and their future schooling outcomes. Effective read-alouds increase children's vocabulary, listening comprehension, story schema, background knowledge, word recognition skills, and cognitive development" (para. 5).

By reading and thinking aloud, the teacher can model the complex processes that happen internally while engaging with text. Students can gain insight into the way a proficient reader reflects, questions, and makes sense of text. This interaction between the reader and the text forms the basis for comprehension. In order to understand a text, proficient readers engage in an ongoing dialogue with it, pausing to think and actively interpret the information they have read. When students receive explicit, direct instruction of various comprehension skills, they develop a toolkit of strategies with which they can effectively interact with different texts.

With reference to some of the various strands of the Reading Rope, read-alouds

- build **background knowledge** and provide opportunities for educators to purposefully plan in ways that honour the learners in their classrooms.
- develop **vocabulary** by exposing students to a wide range of words they would not come across in everyday conversation or books at their decodable level, including Tier 2 and Tier 3 words, which can be explicitly taught and discussed.
- provide opportunities to identify and analyze underlying (text) **language structures**, as well as highlight how syntax (sentence structures) and semantics (meaning of words) convey the meaning of text.
- help students understand how language can be used both literally and figuratively, strengthening their **verbal reasoning** skills through open-ended ques-

> "The practice of a teacher or designated reader orally reading a text with large or small groups. Pictures or text may be shared visually with the students whose primary role is to listen and view the illustrations. The intent is to model proficient reading and language, promote conversation, motivate and extend comprehension and conceptual understandings."
> (International Literacy Association, as cited in Ness, 2024, p. 3)

tions and discussions that allow them to share their interpretations, justify their thinking, and engage in collaborative reasoning.
- allow educators to expose students to a wide variety of **literacy knowledge,** such as text types and genres (novels, informational texts, graphic fiction, newspapers, magazines, encyclopedias, etc.) to support students in identifying print features that help them make meaning of text.
- model fluent reading that supports students' development of **sight recognition** and sufficient fluency, through intonation, expression, and appropriate pacing and phrasing.

It is therefore important for educators to select texts carefully, model explicitly, and intentionally plan opportunities for students to think and share their ideas. McCallum (2020) emphasizes that "well-prepared, purposeful read-alouds are connected to the curriculum, and educators know why they are reading that particular book at that particular time. Thus, purposeful planning will have a profound influence on student achievement" (para. 1).

This also leads to the consideration of *Indigenous Storywork* (Archibald, 2008) and how we need to know when and how it is reasonable and fitting to share a particular story. It is our responsibility as educators to learn and share the diversity of various First Nations, Inuit, and Métis cultures and therefore the multiplicity of Indigenous stories, purposes, and protocols for engaging with them. As Archibald (2008) outlines, stories hold various roles, from sacred traditions and historical record to entertainment. Stories can be healing as individuals are able to interpret and bring meaning to texts in various ways. Furthermore, story ownership can extend from individuals or families or the public and it is vital for educators to understand the principles of Storywork in order to determine whether they can share a particular text. If you take the time to purposefully plan for a read-aloud, you then have the capacity to read and reread the text, allowing students the time they need to think, talk, and make meaning from a story. It is suggested that texts should be shared "a few times before having the children talk about it: They have to know that one day we're going to … look at it [the story]. We're going to lift all the little corners of it" (Archibald, 2008, p. 135). Consequently, make read-alouds an integral component of daily literacy instruction.

DOES WHOLE-CLASS MEAN UNDIFFERENTIATED?

As teachers, we need to differentiate our instruction to suit the needs of all learners in the class. If all instruction were presented in a whole-class fashion, where all students are introduced to a concept and then complete the same task, then one could argue there is little differentiation. However, using whole-class instruction as an integral component in the gradual release of responsibility allows students to gain a shared understanding of the new skills that are being actively introduced.

Differentiated instruction means that each student's strengths and needs are taken into consideration when the teacher plans learning experiences and Purposeful Practice Time, to ensure that each child is challenged and supported in that learning. When planning whole-class learning experiences, the teacher can take into account learning styles and interests of different students, and various strengths and needs.

While most differentiation will happen through small-group instruction, the following elements can apply to all areas of literacy instruction:

- Teachers need to set high expectations for all students, intentionally capitalizing on their strengths rather than focusing on their weaknesses.
- Teachers need to use assessment as a tool to inform instruction. Teachers should use all assessment (before, during, and after) to guide instruction and provide ongoing specific feedback.
- Students should be actively engaged in inquiry to explore important concepts and ideas.
- Tasks need various points of entry and multiple forms of responding to allow students to demonstrate their learning effectively.
- Teachers need to use a variety of instructional approaches to explicitly teach various literacy skills.
- Instructional groupings need to be flexible and responsive, changing frequently to meet the needs and interests of the students. Students can work independently, with a partner, in small groups, or in a whole-class context.
- Teachers should use a range of literacy resources that vary in levels of difficulty and complexity to target students' different reading strengths and areas of need.

Language comprehension strategies can be woven throughout the literacy block to provide students with opportunities to learn through modelled, guided, and independent experiences. Use the Comprehension Time allotted for direct instruction in comprehension when introducing students to a new strategy or reinforcing skills the students have already begun to develop. During this time, you can help the students define the strategy and then you can model how they would use it when reading aloud. Carefully chosen texts and intentionally selected sections are important in allowing students to see the strategy and skills in action. While you are modelling, you might choose a few places in the text to pause and have students share their thinking out loud so that they begin to understand the ways in which a strategy can help when they interpret a text. For example:

This section really helped me visualize what is happening in the book. Listen to the way the author describes the things that we can see and smell in this particular scene.

You can then choose another section of the text and invite students to share the ways in which the comprehension strategy helped them better understand the text. Encouraging students to engage in conversations with each other allows them to become active participants in the comprehension process as they share their thinking and learn from the ideas of their peers.

When you extend the learning into small-group instruction time, students are then provided with the opportunity to practice comprehension strategies in a supported setting. With the guidance of the teacher and in collaboration with their peers, students can apply their learning to a text. While small-group instructions can have many different instructional focuses—including decoding, fluency, and comprehension—they are a perfect time to ensure that students are using comprehension skills and specific strategies in effective ways. In this way, students can transfer their learning from the modelled reading time with the support of an educator (and possibly peers) during targeted, intentional instruction. You can reinforce the students' learning, as well as provide support when it is needed. By engaging students in a respond to text task, you can also to ensure that students are accurately interpreting the text and applying the strategies you have worked on together.

Finally, the students can continue their learning by applying the skills and strategies to their self-selected independent-reading books. When you provide time for students to engage with texts of their choosing and to practice their learning in authentic ways, you allow them to immediately transfer their skills.

When you strategically use the various sections of the literacy block, it becomes possible to seamlessly integrate explicit instruction and the gradual release of responsibility. Twyman (2021) explains that

> Explicit teaching involves guiding student attention and responding toward a specific learning objective within a structured teaching environment. Curriculum content is typically taught in a logical order with the teacher providing demonstration, explanation, and opportunities for practice (often referred to as "Model, Lead, Test," "I do, You do, We do," or some variation)" (para. 20).

Through the vehicles of direct instruction and guided practice in small-groups, students begin to see how they can use their reading response as a way to reflect and share their thinking about the texts with which they are engaged. Responding to texts can also provide a much-needed element of accountability to students' independent reading time. It allows the teacher a greater insight into the students' thinking about the texts they are engaging with, as well as a means of monitoring the ways in which they are applying the skills they are learning.

When building the literacy block or introducing new comprehension tasks, the educator will explicitly and systematically teach students (I Do) how to engage with texts utilizing any number of instructional strategies. Students have the responsibility of actively participating (WE Do) in lessons and various activities to build their knowledge and understanding. This time will then be immediately followed by time for the students to work (YOU Do) on a task assigned by the teacher directly related to the specific skill or strategy the whole class is working through. This creates an intentional sequence of tasks: the teacher actively teaches students a skill through direct instruction and then students are immediately able to practice it on their own. The sequence with which students rotate through the tasks during Purposeful Practice Time will make the difference between busy-work and intentionally applying and practicing the skills they are learning. When responding to texts immediately follows independent and partner reading, students are able to respond to the text as a way of recording and demonstrating their understanding.

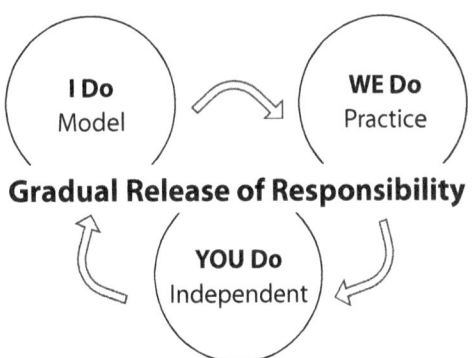

The framework presented in this book naturally lends itself to provide daily opportunities for I Do, WE Do, and YOU Do learning times. Obviously, it would take more than one lesson, and therefore one day, to adequately teach students any of the various comprehension skills and strategies. Flexibility remains the essential element in maintaining a true balance in literacy instruction. Teachers should consider the individual needs of their class when determining how many lessons are needed when targeting the various comprehension skills and strategies.

What Is Text?

What students are reading is as important as *how* students are reading. The term *text* can refer to a wide variety of print, oral, and online media. Comprehension instructional time is an excellent opportunity to engage with a wider variety of texts, such as oral stories, podcasts, visual media such as an infographic, or short films. Our classrooms need to reflect the multimodal environment in which we all live. Messages shared in the media often include complex combinations of words, images, and sounds. If you increase students' experiences to include multiple forms of text, they will gain a better understanding of how to interact with the world through the texts they encounter.

Many students can identify the differences between fiction and nonfiction texts; however, there are different forms of multimodal texts that challenge readers to think critically about the information. Students need to analyze, evaluate, and interpret messages they encounter through various forms of communication. When students are critically literate, they begin to analyze the messages they encounter, asking questions such as these: *Who created the message? Who is the intended audience of the message? Is the message biased in any way? Whose message is being shared? Whose voice is being silenced? What strategies did the author use to engage the audience?* When we include various text forms, we encourage students to consider messages from different perspectives and to think critically about the form, content, and meaning of the texts they are daily bombarded with.

Media literacy is no longer a strand of literacy instruction separate from reading and writing. By including rich media texts as options for read-alouds and independent reading during Comprehension Time, we can model ways of thinking about these different texts as we interact with them. Weaving a variety of texts into small-group instruction and independent reading also provides the time that students need to apply and practice taking their own critical stance on different texts. During small-group or whole-class lessons, consider using a multimodal text, such as a news website, a video, a poster, a commercial, or even graphic text, as a way to frame discussion about these texts.

Analysis of various text forms can also destigmatize the variety of text forms students may choose to engage with when doing independent reading during Purposeful Practice Time. Say it with me: "Audiobooks are real books!" Lane *et al.* (2023) emphasize that "promoting student autonomy through meaningful choices is paramount for fostering intrinsic motivation" (p. 107). By modelling interest and engagement with various text forms, teachers enable students to make choices that will best suit their learning needs. By providing students with the opportunity to choose how they engage with texts during independent reading time (including newspapers, magazines, and links to online resources), educators are likely to increase student engagement and decrease off-task and disruptive behavior (Lane *et al.*, 2023).

During Purposeful Practice Time, technology activities could also include accessing and responding to specific sites or creating texts as a response to reading, viewing, or listening through diverse cross-curricular connections. Unprepared access to the Internet can be overwhelming and potentially disastrous for youngsters. It is highly recommended that teachers take the time to preview sites, texts, and resources before bookmarking or compiling them for easy access on a class website, such as a Google Classroom.

HOT and Critical Literacy

As students begin to think more deeply about texts, they need to rely on higher-order thinking (HOT) skills. This approach to thinking about texts encourages students to question, explore, and reflect on their reading, listening and viewing. When students engage in HOT, they are able to explore plausible answers to questions and defend their ideas with evidence or proof. They can synthesize information from a variety of sources, including their personal experiences, in order to justify their opinion or answer.

In today's world, students are constantly bombarded with different media messages and texts. They need to develop skills to navigate this wide array of information. Developing critical-literacy skills helps students begin to think more deeply about the texts they encounter as well as the texts they create. As a critically literate reader, one is able to read beyond the literal message and think deeply about the text. When we teach students to be critically literate, they understand that texts are written by others and may contain elements of the author's bias. They examine texts in order to understand the author's purpose or intent, to access the underlying messages behind given works, or even to think about whose voices are being represented or silenced. They are given permission to question the authority of texts as they realize that texts reflect the author's beliefs, choices, or positions.

Critical literacy is not a subject; neither is it an element of literacy that stands on its own. It is a lens through which students can learn to view all texts. It should become an integrated component of classroom discussions, an ongoing catalyst for conversations, and a way for students to think and react to different texts.

Talking About Texts

Students should be given frequent opportunities to talk about texts. When students engage in talk, they are processing and integrating their learning in meaningful ways. As Boyd and Markarian (2015) point out, "there is a general consensus that talk and interaction are consequential for learning and that productive learning talk includes joint, critical inquiry and open exchange of ideas" (pg. 274).

However, it is not sufficient to just provide time to talk. For talk to be truly beneficial, it needs to be focused and robust. Students need time to talk about things that are relevant, engaging, challenging, and authentic. We want to fill our learning time with bursts of thoughtful conversations that help propel the learning forward. We need to provide opportunities to talk, give students rich questions and topics to talk about, and create a community where talking-to-learn is the norm.

> **Talk-to-Learn**
>
> Accountable talk is a valuable classroom strategy that encourages students to engage in rich conversations with each other. Janet Allen (2002) suggests that accountable talk can promote cognitive collaboration and active learning; it should be meaningful, respectful, and beneficial to the speaker and the listener. When students communicate, they learn how to articulate their thinking, justify their ideas, and question the opinions of others. Talk can be a powerful vehicle through which students can explore higher-order thinking and inquire collaboratively. Students can communicate, collaborate, question, and explore ideas. When given frequent opportunities for active communication, students develop confidence, are encouraged to take risks, and ultimately learn to express their thinking in complete and sophisticated ways.
>
> Learning is a social process; intentionally orchestrated opportunities to talk allow students to extend their own thinking and the ideas of others. When working as a whole class, students can engage in frequent talk-times to ensure they are actively participating in the learning process. Students use accountable talk as a way to strengthen their understanding through collaboration. They can challenge another's opinion or idea through questioning, or justify their thinking by providing evidence for their ideas. Through talk, students can explore their own ideas more fully as well as build on the ideas of others. Students should feel comfortable sharing opinions and personal perspectives. Accountable talk can be a valuable tool during all areas of literacy instruction, from whole-class instruction to small-group guided sessions. Through ongoing collaboration and purposeful talk-times, students learn how to appreciate differing opinions, disagree respectfully, build on the ideas of others, and integrate new information to enhance their understanding.

According to Boyd and Markarian (2015), talk is vital for the development of certain literacy skills and extrinsically linked to each individual educator:

> Effective teaching and learning are linked to oracy practices in the classroom. The nature, scope, and quality of oracy practices are linked to a teacher's instructional stance, pedagogical flexibility, oral fluency, and willingness to listen and then make decisions about whether and how to bridge what is needed to ready students to connect what they know, to what is being learned (pp. 290–91).

When we think of talk in relation to reading, we realize the need to provide students with opportunities to engage in conversations about texts in a variety of settings. This should include talk-times during direct instruction, small-group conversations during times for targeted instruction, and opportunities to share their thoughts about their reading informally with their peers. Opportunities for talk should be woven throughout the literacy block, fostering a community where students value and respect each other's thoughts, ideas, and opinions.

DEVELOPING A TALK-CENTRED CLASSROOM

When you create a classroom in which students talk-to-learn, it is important to develop a sense of community and mutual respect. Taking time to establish the expectations for talk-times is a valuable investment at the beginning of the year. You can use modelling and direct instruction to help students begin to

Sample Talk-Partner Expectations

I can be a good talk-partner and help support our learning by making sure that we

- sit together and use a quiet voice.
- take turns talking and listening (don't interrupt).
- listen and think about what our partner is saying.
- stay focused and on topic.
- ask our partner to explain their thinking if we don't understand.
- show respect if we disagree or have a different opinion.
- listen with an open mind—listen to understand, not only to respond.
- build on the ideas of our partner.
- use evidence or details to support or explain our ideas.

understand what effective talk-time would look like. They need to understand the role they will play when given opportunities to talk. This might take the form of structured talk opportunities (such as accountable-talk partners during Comprehension Time), group chats during small-group instruction times, or informal partnering during other collaborative learning opportunities. Regardless of when the talk happens or what the talk is about, students need to develop positive habits to ensure that they are getting the most out of their talk-time.

The co-creation of expectations for talk-partners can help guide students when they engage in conversations. Students might find it helpful to role-play the different elements in the expectations or even act out Yes and No examples. In one classroom, students posed for pictures showing each target behavior as both a Yes image and a No image. For example, "We sit close together and use a quiet voice" is illustrated with (a) *Yes!* (image of students sitting side by side) and (b) *No!* (image of the same students reaching across a table with "loud" expressions, appearing to be shouting). These were displayed on a bulletin board and served as visual reminders for students about how to use their talk-times effectively. Not only were these fun to create, they also helped to reinforce the important aspects of how students should use talk to learn.

MAXIMIZING COMPREHENSION THROUGH TALK

Talk is a powerful tool for enabling students to engage with texts, think deeply about different ideas, consider varying perspectives, and provide evidence to justify their thinking or prove their point. Educators are therefore tasked with skillfully supporting and directing students' thinking through discussion, allowing students' academic language to develop naturally and connect their ideas to texts in an intentional way. When educators listen closely to student contributions and are familiar with their curriculum, they can consistently and adaptably connect what students contribute in conversations to the content of the curriculum. This process ultimately makes learning more meaningful for students as the content becomes something they genuinely understand rather than just something the teacher knows (Boyd, M., 2015).

As a class engages with a text, educators can intentionally plan for and weave in opportunities for students to talk with each other about the text. This can be done in a number of ways. Two examples are outlined below.

THINK-ALOUDS DURING DIRECT INSTRUCTION

During direct-instruction times, when you are reading aloud to students, pause occasionally to share your thinking or pose a question. Typically, when you pose a question to the class, the students raise their hands to respond. But what would happen if, when you asked a question, all students were invited to share their answers? Chaos? Not necessarily. If students can share their thinking with a partner, they can all have an opportunity to be heard. In a simple strategy called Think–Pair–Share, students are all given the opportunity to respond to questions posed by the teacher. This approach for incorporating talk into instructional time allows all students to have their voices heard. Simply stated, when reading a text aloud, the teacher pauses to ask the students a question: a question about the text, such as "How is the text organized?" or a verbal reasoning question like "What do you predict will happen next?"; a question that focuses on the author, such as "Why did the author write this text?" or "What authority does the author have to write about this topic?"; or a more complex question about the reader's analysis, such as "What are the potential biases or perspectives presented in the text?"

When provided with two or three opportunities to pause, think, and respond during the reading of a text, students are able to interact with the text, share their thinking, and collaborate with their peers.

INTRODUCING AND SUMMARIZING TEXTS WITH CONSIDERATIONS

When introducing students to a text for a read-aloud lesson, consider framing it with text considerations, such as several questions that support comprehension through background knowledge or vocabulary: "What do students need to know about the topic before engaging with this text?"; "What does the book assume we already know or understand?"; "Are there cultural elements that students may not be familiar with?"; "What words might students not understand?"; "What potential barriers to understanding or points of confusion are there?" These questions are examples of considerations educators must make before engaging with a text with students. For students, posing some questions at the beginning of reading that can be revisited during or after the reading can help to activate and build the background knowledge and vocabulary necessary for students to comprehend the text. Posing questions that require students to reflect on the text as a whole or justify their opinion can also help generate more meaningful conversations than posing questions that can be answered with information explicitly stated in the text. By introducing texts with such considerations, the teacher encourages students to think critically about the information they encounter during the reading. Revisiting the information shared before and during reading also provides students with an opportunity to talk with their partners, sharing their thinking and responding to the ideas of others. This increases student engagement as they become active participants in the lesson. Students can actively engage immediately with the text and with each other in meaningful discussions; they are able to express their own ideas and challenge the ideas of others; they can provide evidence to support their thinking or share personal knowledge that helps justify their responses. By intentionally incorporating talk-times, teachers are able to monitor students' thinking and learning. These brief yet powerful opportunities for talk are critical in helping students become robust thinkers.

Educators can use the samples in the following chart to help students intentionally play for their engagement with texts.

Instead of asking …	Try asking …
• Why did the main character cheat on his test? • How did the main character feel at the end of the book? • What happened when the main character was caught? • What happened when the main character broke the rules? • How did the main character solve the problem? • Which character was your favorite? • Where does the text take place?	• Do you think it is ever okay to cheat on a test? • How do you know the main character learned an important lesson through the book? • Do you think justice was served when the main character was caught? • Is it ever okay to break the rules? • What obstacle do you think was the hardest for the main character to overcome? • If you were the main character, how might you have tried to solve the problem?

- How old do you think the main character is?
- Do you agree with the decisions the main character makes?
- What are some of the traits you admire most about the main character?
- Do you think the main character was treated fairly?
- If this was a real person, would you choose him or her as a friend? Why or why not?
- What audience did the author have in mind when they wrote this book?
- What facts do you think are the most important to remember from this text? Why?
- How do you know if this text is fact or fiction?

Accountable Talk-Partners

As a way to increase accountability, consider intentionally putting students together as talk-partners. By strategically partnering students, you can ensure that all students have an equal opportunity to share and be heard. With intentional talk-partners, you can maximize learning opportunities for all students by strategically separating students when necessary, allowing students to work with a greater variety of peers, and creating thoughtful partnerships from which both partners will benefit.

You might place each student's name on a small card with a magnet on the back. These cards can be displayed in a list on the board, helping students identify their talk-partner. This allows students to sit beside their talk-partners during lessons in order to turn easily and talk with each other. Talk-partners should be changed frequently (daily or weekly) to maximize the level of accountability during partner conversations.

As opportunities for talk are woven throughout the literacy block, students can join in thoughtful conversations during direct instruction, small-group instruction, and collaborative learning. In a community where students use talk as a vehicle for learning, they will have greater opportunities for actively engaging with texts and building on the ideas of others.

WE'RE TALKING DIGITAL

Talk can take many forms. Students can engage in rich conversations face to face. Or they can use digital tools to connect with people outside their school or community, an option that allows them to talk first-hand with experts or learn together with students in other schools, cities, or even countries. As global citizens, students are able to engage in world events and actively communicate with children in other parts of the world. Digital tools can be used in all aspects of a literacy program to support students' comprehension, composition, and communication skills. Using online resources, students can read about current world events, research information, and engage with different forms of text to strengthen and apply their comprehension skills. They can also create and share a variety of compositions in response to the things they are listening to, viewing, and reading. When digital tools are integrated into the literacy block, students can use their time to read, listen, create, share, view, as well as respond to the work of others.

The reality of budget restrictions is a challenge all teachers face. While it would be lovely to have unlimited access to digital tools, we most likely are all struggling to get our hands on them. But when we consider digital literacy and tools as a vehicle for delivering content, rather than a subject itself, it becomes possible to use whatever tools are available in the most effective way. For example, having access to one computer and an LCD projector, the teacher can use online sources as text during direct-instruction times, focusing on the different text features and strengthening students' awareness of text structure. If teachers have access to only a few classroom computers or devices, they can be used during small-group instruction times, possibly to provide the text for discussion. With access to as few as five computers or devices, teachers can create a designated section of Purposeful Practice Time in which students work independently using these tools. Teachers can bookmark sites that students need to visit, download apps that support specific skill development, or provide assignments that require students to create and share media works. There is really no need for a class set of devices or computers.

By integrating media awareness and digital literacy into the literacy block framework (through direct-instruction, small-group, and independent work times), teachers allow students to use the resources available to them in the most effective and efficient manner. As we work our way through the realities and challenges, we need to be flexible and creative to maximize the resources available to our students.

6 Purposeful Practice of Comprehension

As Purposeful Practice Time starts, the students all seem to go in different directions at once. Pausing to consult the tracking board, they gather the materials they require and set off to their designated tasks …

… **Liam** picks up his reading journal and heads to the conference table. Within a few minutes, several of his classmates meet him there and they begin to go through their decoding practice routine. The teacher leads them through the same routine as the previous day's review of multisyllabic word reading to consolidate their learning of vowel team syllables. She also takes a moment to provide feedback on the completed multisyllabic word work from the previous day's lesson. She makes a mental note that Liam has had difficulty with the vowel team /ai/, so she plans to include this in today's small-group encoding practice. The teacher conducts a small-group lesson on encoding the vowel team. She challenges Liam with the word *contain* and asks him to put his finger on the part of the word that has the vowel team. After encoding and decoding a number of words together, the group is dismissed to their desks. They take their work with them and complete the guided practice independently. The teacher has also given them a copy of a decodable text to practice working with multisyllabic words that have vowel teams. The students spend the next 10 to 15 minutes on their tasks or on what they were scheduled to be doing on the tracking board.

… **Marcus** met with the teacher the day before for a reading mini-lesson and was struggling with the concept of determining importance to summarize ideas from a text. As he settles down with his independent reading book, he plans to record three big ideas from this day's reading. The nonfiction book he is reading is full of interesting facts and amazing photographs. Before long, he is fascinated with the bizarre and outrageous information contained in his book. As he reads, he consciously tries to distinguish the difference between big ideas and supporting details. He pulls out his journal and flips to the response task he has chosen to complete. He thinks critically about the content of the book and is certain that he can identify at least two big ideas. He records them, then pauses to come up with a third. As he flips the book shut, an idea dawns on him—the cover image and title help him form a third big idea. Satisfied that he has completed his work to the best of his ability, Marcus eagerly returns to his reading. The random facts are too difficult to resist!

… **Rayan** can't wait for Purposeful Practice Time to begin. He has been watching the schedule in anticipation and today is his day, his favorite day in Literacy World. As soon as the teacher indicates that Purposeful Practice Time is about to begin, Rayan is halfway across the classroom on his way to the computers. He is eager to work on his advertisement, certain to convince everyone that his product is the best and most important invention in the world. Rayan has chosen to create an entire media blitz, including posters, comic strips, and a full 30-second commercial, that is sure to impress. He settles into a focused, engaged trance as his fingers dance across the keyboard. When the teacher gives the signal to change tasks, Rayan smiles, knowing that he has more time to continue working on his media blitz.

... Before she begins Purposeful Practice Time, **the teacher** takes a moment to review the daily tracking board to ensure that all students know which tasks they will be working on and in what order. She invites a few students to meet with her first so she can do a targeted decoding lesson. Today her group is small as she only has three students working on the decoding pattern *consonant + le*. She asks them to bring their reading journals with them, and also reminds the students working on other tasks to use the Waiting Room if they have any questions during her small-group lesson. The groups are all dismissed and they head to their respective tasks. She notices that Scarlett has paused to review the modelled composition task and that Rayan is so eager he almost trips over the carpet. By the time the teacher gets to the conference table, Liam and his group have already gathered and started to share their decoding and encoding work from the day before. She takes a few moments to review their work, providing immediate feedback and making a note of areas that each student needs to continue working on. Liam and two other students in the group are struggling with the vowel team /ai/; this will certainly be an instructional focus for today's lesson.

Once the decoding lesson has concluded, the teacher walks around the room to check in with students as they work on their various tasks. No one was using the Waiting Room, but she noticed that Sophia has been slow to start the last couple times and pauses to touch base with her. After a brief one-on-one conference, she signals to the students to change to their second task. She can't help but notice the ear-to-ear grin on Rayan's face!

The teacher now invites a couple of the students who have been working on their independent compositions to the conference table. Once the conferences are over and the young writers head back to their desks, the teacher glances at the clock and notices that Purposeful Practice Time has come to an end. She signals the class to finish their tasks and gather for Comprehension Time. Rayan is still smiling!

From Comprehension Time to Independent Reading

The cornerstone to an effective literacy block is structuring opportunities for small-group instruction. Through frequent small-group meetings or conferences, the teacher is able to constantly assess each student's learning as well as immediately identify gaps or areas for further growth and development. Through students' Purposeful Practice Time, teachers can find the time they need to provide this targeted instruction and intervention that meet students' individual needs.

As you build the literacy block (see Chapter 2), students develop an understanding that there are times when they may be learning by completing a range of tasks. For example, one group of students might be working on independent reading while another is working on partner reading, or some students might be engaging in small-group instruction while others are completing a response task independently. The structure shared in this book differs from other models of literacy instruction in the intentionality with which students' independent work is connected to the learning that happens during other times in the literacy block. Students take time to work on responding to texts directly following independent comprehension time. This allows them to immediately apply and practice the lessons they have learned throughout the week during Comprehension Time. As students rotate through the different elements of Purposeful Practice Time, they move simply and seamlessly from whole-class and small-group instruction to independent practice and back.

As we work through the various layers of the Literacy Block—Composition, Comprehension—we must remind ourselves that Structured Literacy and Multi-Tiered Systems of Support (MTSS) mean much more than maintaining a daily schedule for literacy. The key is to ensure we are providing the right support to the right students at the right time. Therefore, the structure or routine that we construct is paramount to our ability to provide instruction and interventions when our students need it.

Comprehension Cycle

At the beginning of the year, imagine reading aloud from your favorite picture book to your students and sharing a think-aloud lesson. During this lesson, you make your thinking visible to the students. They hear your thoughts as you talk about the connections you are making and the important ideas you identify in the text. The conversation throughout the lesson encourages students to share and to use their knowledge to enhance their comprehension of the text. Upon completion of the lesson, students apply what they have learned in the lesson they have just participated in. They may complete a Venn diagram to identify similarities and differences between the text they have just read and another one, or perhaps they write a reflection about how the author's word choice helped them paint a picture in their mind. Whatever they choose to do, they have had an opportunity to participate in focused instruction and converse with peers, followed immediately by an opportunity to apply and practice this learning.

Fast-forward a bit and consider how students can intentionally work to build their fluency skills along with their comprehension skills, in order to make the most of the time in your literacy block. It's time to introduce Partner Reading. This cooperative learning strategy and intervention involves pairs of students collaboratively reading a text by taking turns reading aloud and giving constructive feedback to one another (Vaughn *et al.*, 2022). After explicitly modelling the strategy with student volunteers (or another educator), teachers can work with students to co-create anchor charts to support their effective participation in partner reading throughout the year. Over several days, with an instructional focus in mind, students are given the opportunity to practice the strategy with mixed-ability partners selected by the teacher. To help monitor their comprehension, students are invited to complete a summarizing task to share the main ideas from the text they have read together. Perhaps this is something they do in their reading journal or even in a podcast style posted to Google Classroom or another online learning platform. Whatever you feel is the best way to engage your students will work and can also evolve over time.

The class has now had an opportunity to practice their fluency and comprehension skills in a very scaffolded manner using texts and partners the teacher has selected. Following this, using books that they have chosen, students have the chance to read independently and apply their learning to a new text of their choice. This is independent reading time. For example, one student has selected a picture book, another a nonfiction text, and another an online article that she listens to on a class laptop computer. These students continue to think about how they can strengthen their comprehension by applying the learning to their self-selected texts. To monitor their own learning, the students can complete a simple reflection task to show how they were thinking while they were reading.

SAMPLE COMPREHENSION PURPOSEFUL PRACTICE TIME

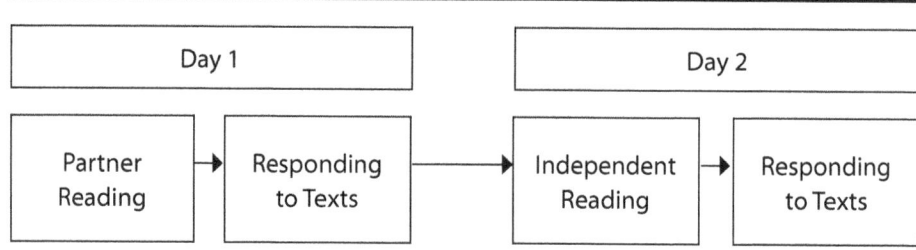

In this simple framework, it is easy to see the gradual release of responsibility at work. Students spend time working with the teacher in a focused group lesson to learn a new skill or continue to build on an existing one. The next day, they apply their learning to a new text and continue to expand their learning with a partner. When these students then have the opportunity to engage with texts independently, they can more confidently attempt to apply the skills they have had the chance to practice. In subsequent lessons, the teacher can assess the learning that the students have done based on how they demonstrated their thinking through the two different responses, as well as through the observations and conversations that take place during the partner reading opportunities. Simply put, the teacher can triangulate the assessment, using observations, conversations, and products, to quickly assess student learning. This opportunity for ongoing assessment and feedback lets the teacher begin each lesson with a review/recap of the students' learning from the previous session, assess the students' progress, and use this to inform further instruction.

Constructing Purposeful Practice Time

You can't begin to build an independent comprehension routine without first considering how students are going to read and engage with texts. While selecting books is an important skill (and definitely one that needs to be addressed), it might not be essential for you to help with it on the first day. As the literacy routines continue to develop and deepen, there will be plenty of opportunities for direct instruction on how to select books, abandon books, and so on. However, to initiate the purposeful practice of comprehension and to build students' stamina, you might allow them time to peruse the classroom library, preview audiobooks and podcasts they have access to, and select a few texts that seem interesting to them.

> **A Note about Independent Reading**
>
> Encouraging students to immerse themselves in independent reading practice can spark their interest and motivation and nurture their growth as learners who use reading to gain knowledge and understanding of the world around them. This being said, independent reading practice cannot replace a comprehensive reading program in fostering the development of skilled readers. Bus, Shang, and Roskos (2024) explain that
>
> > IR [Independent Reading] should be an essential component of the reading curriculum and a regular practice in reading pedagogy. ... However, it is important to remember that IR is not intended to replace teacher-led reading instruction. Instead, it serves as a complementary activity that enhances students' engagement with reading, making it indispensable not only for supporting reading skill development but also for fostering a love of reading (p. 14).
>
> This important distinction that independent reading practice supplements, but does not replace, direct instruction in reading is vital to ensuring all students have equitable access to learning to read and that the burden of learning to read is not placed on the child. As we saw in the Reading Rope, students must develop a number of skills to become skilled readers. The word recognition (decoding) side of the Reading Rope is especially important to consider when planning independent reading tasks. If a student cannot access "the code" (cannot lift the words off the page), then no matter how well developed their language comprehension skills, they will not be able to engage with written text independently. This is when targeted intervention provided through small-group instruction will be vital for students learning to decode.
>
> So how do my students who cannot decode at grade-level engage in independent reading? It is my responsibility to use a Universal Design for Learning (UDL) and provide multiple means of access for my students so they are able to practice comprehension tasks independently in a purposeful and differentiated way. When we offer them various forms of text (novels, graphic novels, audiobooks, podcasts, videos, infographics, and so on), all students can engage in purposeful independent practice of comprehension skills and strategies. I can then plan for small-group intervention and targeted instruction to build students' decoding skills to work towards closing the gaps in word recognition skills. This is also when knowing and understanding curriculum expectations will be vital for assessing students' comprehension to inform further instructional opportunities.

Building Stamina—Comprehension Routine

There are many different ways to organize classroom libraries and resources. I have found that using magazine boxes to group texts into categories lets students easily locate those of interest to them. Leading up to the launch of your independent comprehension routine, provide students with browsing time to select up to five texts they can place in a personalized book box. Magazine boxes work perfectly for this purpose too, as students can use them to house all of their literacy materials in one place. Encourage each student to choose a range of texts (for example, two picture books, one or two nonfiction texts, a magazine, and a graphic novel) and place them in their book box. This way, students already have a wide selection of texts to choose from when you are ready to begin the routine, and they can engage with a text for the required length of time. If you have technology for students to access audiobooks and podcasts, ensure you have clear expectations and a routine to support their access to these resources.

If you are planning on initiating your comprehension routines in the first few days of school, also consider including an exploration of the classroom library and digital devices available to students as a "welcome" activity for your new class. It might be a nice way to get to know your youngsters by asking them to share the reasons they are attracted to the texts they have chosen (Nate has chosen a nonfiction book about trucks because he likes Mighty Machines; Radhija has chosen a graphic novel about Pokémon because she loves to collect cards; Amanda has selected to listen to an audiobook she started over the summer and hasn't had a chance to finish yet; and so on).

DAY ONE

(Instructional time: approximately 25 minutes)
Begin by gathering the students together as a large group.

Learners! Today we are going to start something really important. It is really important because it will help us all learn and work together all year. We are going to start our independent comprehension practice today. Think for a moment. Why do you think reading is important?

Allow students a few moments to think about this question.

Perhaps you can tell someone beside you why you think reading is important.

Encourage students to turn to a partner and share their ideas. After they have had an opportunity to talk with a partner, select a few students to share their responses with the whole class. As they share, record their thinking on chart paper to keep for later reference.

Yes, I agree that reading is very important. In fact, we all learn a lot from engaging with various texts! We can read nonfiction books to find out information; we can listen to fiction books to help us imagine new and exciting things; or we could even examine a poster or infographic to find out new information. Reading is very important. But how can we learn to be better readers?

Again, encourage students to share their ideas with a partner and then with the whole class, recording their ideas on a chart that might look like this one.

SAMPLE CHART: COMPREHENSION INDEPENDENT PRACTICE

Why is reading important?	What would it look like?
• We learn things from reading. • It helps to teach us new words. • We can stretch our imagination. • It helps us find answers to our questions.	• Everyone has a text they are looking at. • Everyone stays in the spot they chose. • Our eyes would be on the text we are examining. • We would see headphones or earphones on people listening to texts.
How can we learn to be better readers?	What would it sound like?
• We can learn how to decode longer and harder words. • We can read faster. • We can practice thinking while we read or listen to a text. • We can read with more expression. • We can work with our teacher or classmates to practice our reading.	• It would be really quiet. • We would all be reading and thinking in our heads. • We might hear whispering if someone reads aloud, but they stay quiet.

There are lots of things we can do to become better readers. One really important thing we need to do is practice our comprehension independently. This means thinking about our texts and reading on our own. When we practice independent comprehension, we are enjoying our texts by ourselves and allowing our friends to enjoy their texts by themselves. Reading is hard work, and we need to make sure that we are thinking while we engage with texts to make sure that we understand the things being shared by the author. We also want to make sure that our friends are able to read their texts. We need to be really quiet so that we can all enjoy our time. What do you think it would look like and sound like in our classroom if everyone were reading their texts independently?

Encourage students to share their ideas and then record their suggestions about what it might look like and sound like.

Our brains are a little like our muscles. If we want them to get strong, we need to exercise them. But when we do exercises, we need to start slowly and gradually do more and more until our muscles are strong. Well, our "comprehension muscles" are kind of like that. We are going to start building our muscles today. We are going to use the texts we have chosen to practice independently for three minutes. After three minutes, we will come back together to share some of the things we have thought about on our own.

Answer any questions that the students have. Ensure that they are all in appropriate places, have their texts, and are ready to begin.

Readers, we are going to read for three minutes, starting now.

During this time, stand or sit in a place where you can see the students but are not a focus of their attention. It is not a good idea to wander among the students. The best place to sit is at the table you will use for your small-group instruction and intervention. Students will get used to the idea that you are nearby but not hovering.

Once three minutes have elapsed, gently redirect the students, letting them know that their time is up.

You have worked independently for three minutes. Please get to a place where you can stop—the end of a sentence or paragraph—and be ready to come back together as a class.

If you are using talk-partners, encourage students to find a place to sit with them and bring the text they were engaging with.

I'm sure you all learned many interesting or exciting things during this time. Take a few minutes and share with a partner something interesting that you found.

Allow students a few minutes to share their texts—talking about a favourite picture, an interesting idea, or the funny part that they just have to share.

How did you feel about reading for three minutes? Do you think that you can read for a little bit longer next time? Tomorrow, our goal will be to practice independent comprehension for five minutes. For now, please put your texts and devices away so that you will have them when you need them again.

Well done! You are beginning to put in place the key foundations of a literacy block that includes the components necessary for incorporating Structured Literacy. By dedicating time to build routines for independent reading, you help students recognize that their Purposeful Practice Time holds as much value as the time they spend learning with you. These routines provide opportunities for students to apply, practice, and strengthen the skills and strategies they have learned throughout the other elements of the literacy block. Independent work is not optional or secondary. It is a powerful way for students to take charge of their own learning and work toward personal goals.

DAY TWO AND BEYOND

Begin the second day of building independent reading routines by reviewing the charts you constructed with the students. If they have any additions or changes they would like to make, be sure to add them to the charts so they can continue to be working documents as you establish routines. It is vital that students take ownership of the Purposeful Practice Time as it is valuable and productive time that supports each learner in reaching their individual goals. Students might wish to share some of the things they enjoyed or discovered during their independent reading time, such as an interesting fact they read or an idea that they were excited to continue hearing about in their next podcast episode.

Over the next week, repeat the procedure, taking a few minutes each day to review the charts, answer questions, and address any challenges students might be facing. Gradually increase the time the students spend working independently until they are able to complete Purposeful Practice Time independently for the desired length of time. This target will vary according to the age of the students and their individual needs, but 15 to 20 minutes is a reasonable goal.

As students become more comfortable with the routine of working independently, they need to understand that during this time you will be working with other students. At first, they might find this distracting; they might pause while working to observe or listen to the conversation you are having with other students. Over time, students will learn that everyone's work is important, both the work they are doing independently and the work that others might be doing with the teacher.

Scholars! You have all been working hard to build up your stamina when working independently. Today while you are working, I am going to ask a few people to work with me at our conference table. We will be using whisper-voices so that we don't disturb you. You need to keep doing your work because we all have very important jobs to do. I promise that everyone will have a chance to work with me at the conference table. But when it is not your turn, you need to be working on your own important thinking.

Keys to Success: Independent Reading Time
- Students can self-select independent comprehension options (for example, school or classroom library routine, tools for audiobooks and other digital literature).
- Students can select an appropriate area to work independently.
- Students understand the purpose and value of working independently.
- Stamina is built until students can work independently for 15 to 20 minutes.
- Students can independently solve problems that might arise; for example, they can solve unfamiliar words (decoding) without asking, or ignore distractions that occur.
- Students can access resources, if necessary, including a variety of text options and technology should they need it.
- A washroom procedure is established that allows students to go when necessary without needing to ask the teacher, such as signing out or putting a washroom pylon on their desk.
- Students have opportunities for sharing periodically.

You might wish to use this first time to read one-on-one with students to begin to assess their individual strengths and needs. If you usually complete a reading assessment screener, you might use this time to complete an oral reading fluency assessment with students. Continue to reinforce the importance of the work that students are doing, both independently and at the conference table with you.

Once you have completed your initial reading assessments and the students have had sufficient time to develop the routines of independence, you are ready to start using this time to conduct small-group interventions and instruction. You have already started gathering data through observations, you've had a chance to listen to each child read orally, and you might even have completed a diagnostic reading assessment for students who need it. Forming small groups for instruction is the next logical step, and now you have time in your literacy block designed to accommodate this.

Responding to Texts—Comprehension Routine

Now that we have established independent reading as a part of Purposeful Practice Time, we are ready to introduce students to responding to texts during the Comprehension Time of the literacy block.

One of the biggest challenges we face as teachers is assessment of independent reading. When students are reading independently, we can observe the way they interact with texts, whether they stick with various books or frequently abandon them. We can observe if they seem engaged or not by whether they are actively immersed in them. We can observe their body language and draw informed conclusions about their habits. However, the internal processes that students use when comprehending—the thinking part of comprehending—are more difficult for us to assess. How do we know what students are thinking? How can we be sure the strategies we have been actively teaching them are actually being transferred to their independent reading time? Is there a way to monitor their thinking when they are engaging with texts on their own?

While small-group instruction sessions and conversations we have with students about their reading provide some insight into their thinking, there remains the challenge of monitoring students' thinking and the transfer of their learning to their independent reading time. How can we guide their learning when they are all reading different texts? Is it possible to ensure that students are actively practicing the skills they are learning through other aspects of literacy time? Is there a way that we can monitor and assess this to drive instruction further and guide students' learning?

The most effective way to monitor students' independent reading is through the use of responses to text. Through a range of tasks, students can be encouraged to reflect on their reading and share their thinking in a way that can be easily monitored. There have been many different models for creating written responses to text, including reading-response journals, letters between students and teachers, and other variations. Over the years, I have found that the most effective way to encourage students to reflect on their reading is to use a range of different tools, prompts, and response modes.

At first, you might find it beneficial to introduce students only to a limited number of response formats so that they can develop an understanding of the requirements of each task and the way it will work in their literacy routines. In my experience, when students respond to reading using the same format, initially they are excited to embrace the new approach, but the routine becomes stale as the year goes on. It is important to constantly revisit the tasks that students are using to ensure that they are still engaged while also increasing the complexity and selections of tasks that students can complete. While the action of responding to texts will remain essential throughout the year, teachers should consider embedding elements of choice and using a range of tools through which students may respond. For example, students can select from a range of Response Cards (see pages 115–120) to create a written response, or educators may also consider using various digital tools to enable students to exercise their digital literacy skills to respond to an assortment of texts. In this way, throughout the year students will experience a variety of ways to share their thinking about the texts they are engaging with.

Regardless of the form the reading response takes, it provides students with the much-needed time to practice, consolidate, and apply the skills that have been actively taught during the instructional portions of the literacy block. Allowing students to choose their own texts and the way in which they would like to respond to them ensures differentiation for all students based on their interests, as well as on strengths and needs. Responding to texts provides students with a purpose for their new learning and strengthens their skills. Finally, it provides us with countless opportunities to assess students' learning and thinking. With this information, we can shape our instruction more purposefully.

DAY ONE

(Instructional time: approximately 25 minutes)
Begin by gathering the students as a large group.

> *We have been working really hard to develop our comprehension and composition skills. We have had opportunities to engage with texts independently, and we have all had a turn to read with the teacher. But, as I was watching you, I started to wonder what you were thinking while you were immersed in your various text choices. Can you think for a moment about some of the things you think about when you are reading independently?*

Allow students a few moments to think about this question, then encourage them to share their ideas with a partner. Depending on students' ages and previous reading experiences, their responses will vary greatly. Share with students some of the things that you think about when you are reading. For example, you might say, "When I'm reading a very exciting book, I feel like I'm watching a movie in my head. I can imagine the characters and sometimes I even think that I know what their voices sound like."

When I am thinking really hard, it is impossible for you to see the work that I am doing in my head. And when you are thinking really hard, it is impossible for me to see the work that you are doing in your head. That is why we will use responding to texts tasks as a way for you to share your thinking when you are engaging with texts. Why do you think it is important for you to share your thinking with me?

Allow students to share their ideas with their partners, then select a few students to share their ideas with the whole class.

There are many different ways that we can share our thinking about our reading. What are some of the ways that we can respond to texts?

Again, allow students time to reflect and share their ideas. As they share, record their thinking on chart paper or an interactive whiteboard for later reference.

SAMPLE CHART: SHARING OF COMPREHENSION IDEAS

Why are reading responses important?	What are some ways that we can respond to texts?
<ul><li>We can share the thinking that is happening in our heads.</li><li>The teacher can make sure we are understanding the things that we are reading.</li><li>We can practice the things we are learning with our own books.</li></ul>	<ul><li>Draw pictures.</li><li>Create digital media.</li><li>Write about our thinking.</li><li>Talk about our thinking.</li></ul>

Today, I am going to show you one way that you might share your thinking.

Model a responding to texts task. Begin by sharing the task with students and ask them to keep it in mind as you read a text. Read aloud to the students, pausing to reflect, share your thinking, and pose questions for the students to think and talk about. After sharing, model how you might complete the responding to texts task. You might wish to explicitly draw their attention to important elements in your response (providing evidence from the text, giving examples, drawing on prior experiences, making connections, and so on).

You can see that this responding to texts task helps you see the things that I am thinking when I am reading. The next time we meet for small-group instruction, we are going to do a response together. We are going to use the text that we have read together, and then we can use a response task to show our thinking.

Depending on the age and ability of the students, you might model responses a number of times before beginning to introduce the responding to texts tasks through small-group instruction. Younger learners might benefit from seeing the same (or similar) response modelled repeatedly with different texts, whereas older students would be more likely to respond to the modelling of a greater variety of tasks. As always, it is important to consider each group of learners when establishing and developing elements of the literacy block.

MOVING BEYOND DAY ONE

As students become more comfortable with the requirements of responding to texts tasks through modelling and small-group instruction, they will be better able to transfer these skills to their independent reading texts. At first, it is beneficial for students to be introduced to a responding to texts task through direct instruction. This allows them time to think and collaborate on ways in which they can respond. For example, during small-group instruction, students might be presented with the responding to texts task of visualizing a character. Students could use a shared text to think, talk, and respond to this particular task. On the following day, the students then continue to extend and apply their learning by completing the same responding to texts task in relation to their own independent text, thereby using their ability to visualize a character from a text they have selected themselves.

As they become accustomed to this routine, a visual tracking board might help students stay organized. This will make it easy for them to see which literacy elements they are working on, and when. The board might look a little like this:

SAMPLE TRACKING BOARD: COMPREHENSION PURPOSEFUL PRACTICE, DAY 1

Group	First I will …	Then I will …
Group 1	Partner Reading	Responding to Texts

SAMPLE TRACKING BOARD: COMPREHENSION PURPOSEFUL PRACTICE, DAY 2

Group	First I will …	Then I will …
Group 1	Independent Reading	Responding to Texts

The gradual release of responsibility is created by initially working with students directly through whole-class instruction and immediately following with a respond to texts task. Then, students have the opportunity to practice their response skills with a partner to consolidate their learning. During this time, the teacher may also pull small groups for instruction if needed to help guide their practice. The following day, students apply and transfer their learning by reading independently (or listening to reading to differentiate for students who are not able to decode at grade level) and completing another responding to texts task for a self-selected text. This lets them immediately transfer the skills learned through whole-class and small-group instruction to their independent reading texts.

Once students are comfortable with this routine, it becomes possible to focus more on a particular topic to build consensus and consistent background knowledge with the class in order to more effectively model and teach the application of various strategies and skills while reading. Teachers can then present students with a selection of responding to texts tasks to choose from to respond to their independent texts. In this way, students can apply something they have learned through modelled and targeted instruction, then transfer it to their own reading.

A simple classroom organizational tool you might find helpful is an interactive bulletin board with pockets on it. Each pocket can be labelled with a specific comprehension strategy or skill and contain a variety of response templates specifically designed to target that strategy or skill. A digital option might be to include links to the tasks on a class website or Google Classroom. Students are able to self-select a responding to texts task that will strengthen the skills they have been working on through whole-class and small-group instruction, and they can begin to apply and transfer these skills through partner and independent reading. You may also consider inviting students for small-group instruction where they bring their completed responses to share with the group. This would provide an easy way to monitor and assess students' learning and use this information to guide further discussions and instructional time. Students also have the opportunity to share their work with the teacher and their peers and receive feedback to improve their continued purposeful practice.

While the structure provided on the Responding to Texts task cards can be helpful to some students, others might prefer to respond by writing in a journal. Teachers can provide journals in which each student can either write or glue in the task cards they have selected to complete. For younger students, you might even find it helpful to enlarge the task cards. The Responding to Texts tasks provided on pages 115–120 can be used as a starting point: you might change or add to them in order to cater to the individual learning needs of your specific class. The tasks can be used in a variety of ways as students respond to their independent or partner reading texts and should serve as a starting point, regardless of which form they may take. Worksheets and task cards do not replace necessary reading instruction and should be used to complement a comprehensive, structured literacy block.

At the end of the day, the key to success with any instructional framework is flexibility. Teachers need to adjust their instruction based on the needs and dynamics of an individual class. The literacy framework in this book provides a structure that teachers can use and adapt to best suit the needs of their individual classes. Reading for enjoyment should have a place in ongoing literacy routines to maximize student engagement. We see that responding to texts help teachers monitor and assess students' reading and thinking, which in turn helps to inform future instruction. These exercises have a valuable place in regular literacy routines; however, there should be times when teachers encourage students to read for enjoyment, without the need to formulate a formal response. If you build in opportunities for choice, both within tasks and in the selection of tasks, you will ensure that student engagement is heightened.

Do I Have to Mark Everything They Read and Respond To?

In short, no. Although you might feel like you need to evaluate all student work, it is important to remind ourselves why we are doing what we do. *Growing Success* (2010) states that "the primary purpose of assessment and evaluation is to improve student learning" (p. 6). If your assessment practices are not in line with this pedagogy, then it is time to stop and think. Assessment *for* Learning—that is, assessment that guides and informs our instruction—should integrate seamlessly with your instruction to be most effective. Brainstorming, warm-ups, and other purposeful practice activities should not be formally evaluated but rather assessed *for* learning in order not to penalize students for not knowing or understanding content before or during a period of instruction. Teachers can use such strategies as sharing learning goals and success criteria, providing timely feedback, and developing students' ability to self-assess in order to monitor and communicate a student's progress toward achieving learning goals. (We will discuss efficient practices for this in Chapter 8.)

Embedding Digital Literacy and Cross-curricular Learning

Technology and the use of digital tools in the classroom are not extra or optional features. They are powerful tools that should be woven seamlessly into the literacy program. Critical thinking and digital literacy skills enhance and extend student learning by reinforcing the skills and content already being taught. When used intentionally, they become a natural part of instruction, supporting students in developing deeper understanding, practicing essential skills, and engaging in authentic learning experiences.

Our classrooms are no longer limited to the four walls within which the desks are confined. Digital tools and resources are an essential component for communication; as teachers, we need to address the critical thinking and digital literacy skills associated with their use. Embracing Tech Time doesn't need to be scary though! The use of technology in our classrooms allows us to enhance student engagement, foster autonomy, promote higher-order thinking, and support our students in making meaningful connections to other content areas and the world around us. By intentionally planning and integrating tasks that make use of various digital tools and resources into the literacy block, we are better equipped to teach students to evaluate, integrate, and consolidate their learning.

Tech Time Cycle

The tasks during Tech Time can vary greatly and may include writing a blog post, viewing a video, reading a website, creating a work of media, publishing final writing tasks; the possibilities are endless! However, access to technological devices may not be endless, so teachers must take this into account when planning for this time in their literacy block. You do not need a device for each student for this kind of work to take place! Nonetheless, you need at least a couple working devices that are charged and ready for student use.

In my own practice, this is always the last piece of the Purposeful Practice Time puzzle to come together, mainly because it often requires extensive preparation, explicit modelling, and the building of background knowledge for students to get it rolling effectively. The tasks assigned invite students to apply skills they are still developing at the beginning of the school year, and they require subject-specific knowledge to make sense. For example, a task may ask students to watch a short video or read an article about a topic we are studying in another content area in order to apply the elements of the inquiry process (formulating questions, gathering information, organizing findings, evaluating and drawing conclusions, and communicating findings). In recording their response to the task, students are applying various literacy skills in order to demonstrate an understanding of a concept or content from a specific subject area.

Some examples of ways in which you can use Tech Time:

- Creative publishing platforms allow students to create trailers or digital storyboards to demonstrate comprehension of a text.
- Online libraries, e-books, and digital articles can provide a wider range of materials than traditional print resources alone. Students can therefore explore current news articles or global perspectives on topics from a variety of disciplines.
- Extending the learning beyond the classroom with opportunities such as virtual field trips bring disciplinary literacy to life.

Caution: Consider the protection of students' personal data and consult with your board's digital literacy policies to ensure you are in accordance.

- Digital platforms allow students to share ideas, give feedback, and publish their work for authentic audiences by using collaborative documents for peer editing or posting reflections on a class website.
- Evaluating online sources and understanding media supports the development of critical digital literacy skills, as students compare various websites for credibility as part of a research project.

In this manner, students can use their Purposeful Practice Time to integrate a wide range of digital literacy skills into content areas within and beyond the literacy block.

Putting It All Together

Now that we have identified and introduced the various components that can be used to build Purposeful Practice Time, we can structure them to support our ability to scaffold learning so it is intentionally connected to learning happening during other times in the literacy block. Purposeful Practice Time is not busy-work planned separately from the content of other lessons and activities happening during the literacy block. The practice students engage in makes up highly scaffolded supports and extensions of the learning so teachers can easily differentiate instruction for the variety of learning needs in any given classroom.

Here is a tracking board like the ones you saw in Chapter 2. Rotate through the cycle either by moving groups up or moving activities down.

SAMPLE TRACKING BOARD

Group	First I will …	Then I will …
Group 1	Independent Reading	Responding to Texts
Group 2	Partner Reading	Responding to Texts
Group 3	Words Skills	Transcription Practice

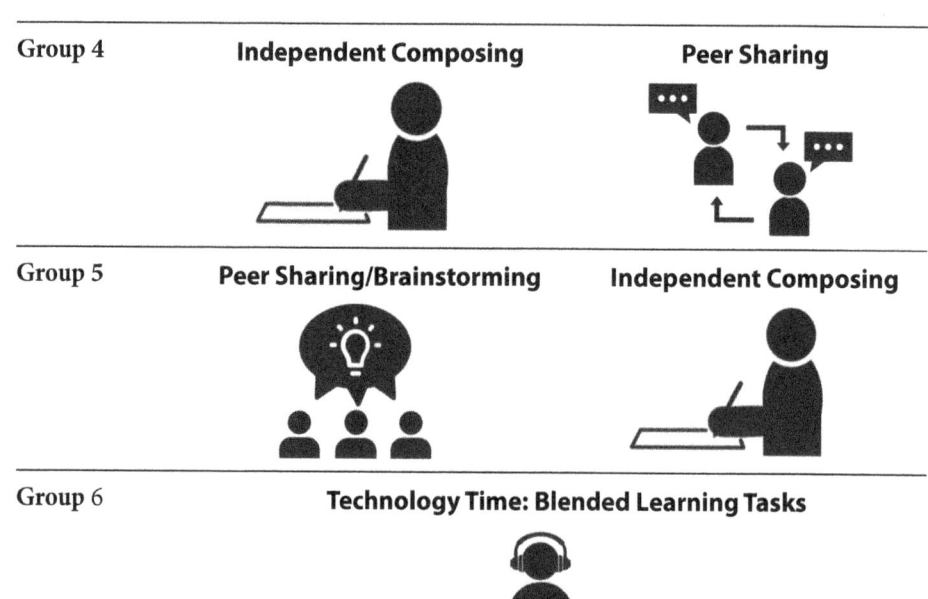

When you take the time to ensure the routines are solidly established, everyone greatly benefits throughout the year. Students will use this time to practice and apply the skills they are learning and to set and monitor their personal learning goals. Still, it might be necessary periodically to revisit the charts created during the early development of the literacy block. As the year progresses, the literacy block will continue to build. Layer upon layer, students will engage in additional tasks. Regardless of other routines added to the literacy block, the foundation remains the same. Solid independent routines provide students with the time necessary to firmly apply and consolidate their learning. In this practice time, students will combine the skills they are actively learning with their personal interests and choices to make their learning relevant, authentic, and purposeful.

Purposeful Practice Time provides teachers with valuable opportunities to meet with small groups of students and provide necessary interventions, valuable instruction, and immediate feedback on their reading, writing, and thinking. It allows students to transfer and apply the learning that happens during Composition Time, Comprehension Time, and during whole-class and small-group instruction. It is based on providing authentic tasks that encourage students to engage in purposeful learning. Providing choice, through responding to texts tasks, composition prompts and ideas, along with digital tasks, ensures that students have a voice, not only in what they are learning, but also in how they demonstrate that learning. By introducing each of the elements through Composition Time and Comprehension Time, teachers set the stage for students to use their time to maximize their learning. Finally, strategically scheduling the elements of Purposeful Practice Time enables students to immediately transfer and apply learning as they alternate between independent work, collaborative activities, and opportunities for small-group instruction.

Responding to Texts Task Cards

MORPHOLOGY

Morpheme Hunt

Become a morpheme collector by hunting for all the words in a passage of your text that use the following suffixes. Keep a record of your words in the chart to see how many you can find!

-ed	-ly	-ful

MORPHOLOGY

Word Sums

Find five words and create word sums to show how the words are built.

Example: re + build + ing = rebuilding

VOCABULARY

Glossary

Create a glossary of new vocabulary that you've learned while engaging with a passage in your text. Beside each word, write its meaning. You might need to check in a dictionary or with another source to verify that you're sure what the word means.

VOCABULARY

Word Choice

Find a passage from the text that shows how the author used their choice of words to help share the message. It might be a very descriptive part of a story or a very informative section of a nonfiction resource. Which **Tier 2** vocabulary (words) were the most powerful to you as the reader?

Responding to Texts Task Cards

STRATEGIC THINKING

5 Senses
Choose a really descriptive passage from your text. Try to describe it using as many senses as possible.

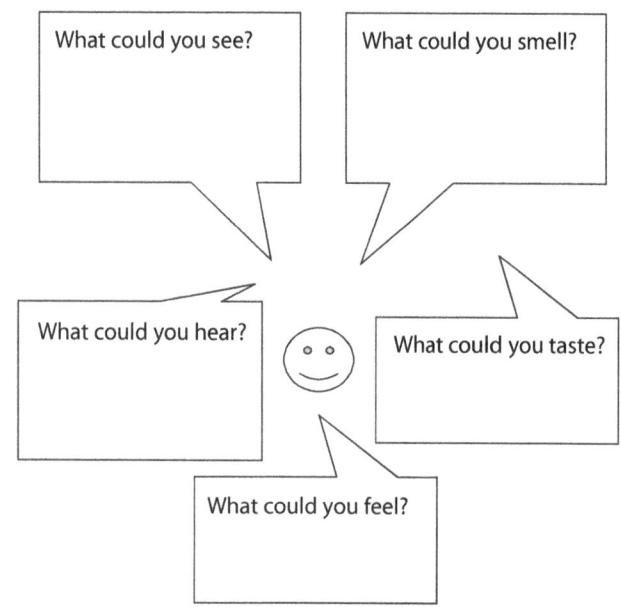

STRATEGIC THINKING

Words Have Power!
Select a part of the text that you were able to visualize clearly. Draw an image to share your thinking. Include evidence from the text that supports your picture.
The text said

_____
_____
_____
_____

In my mind I imagined

STRATEGIC THINKING

What's Most Important?
Choose three important ideas from the text. Put them in order from the most important to the least important. Explain why you thought each idea belonged where you put it.

	Ideas from the Text	Rationale
Least Important Idea ↕ Most Important Idea		

STRATEGIC THINKING

Sequencing Ideas
Summarize three of the most important ideas from the text. Use sequencing words to show the order in which the events occurred.

Responding to Texts Task Cards

STRATEGIC THINKING

Ask the Characters
Imagine you are able to meet the characters from the text. What questions would you ask them?

Character	Questions I would like to ask

STRATEGIC THINKING

Finding the Answers
What questions did you have as you were reading the text? If you were able to find the answers, record them so you can share them with a friend.

Questions I had:	Answers I discovered:

STRATEGIC THINKING

In My Life ...
Does this text remind you of something you have personally experienced? Have you been in a similar situation, met a similar person, or been to a similar place? Describe how your experiences are similar to the text.

_____
_____
_____
_____
_____
_____
_____

STRATEGIC THINKING

The Text Made Me Think
Complete the chart, showing the connections you made while reading.

Ideas I connected with	These ideas made me think of...

Responding to Texts Task Cards

STRATEGIC THINKING

Author's Intent
What do you think was the author's purpose when they wrote this text? What was the message they wanted to share with you? Use information from the text to support your thinking.

___

STRATEGIC THINKING

Character's Thoughts!
Are there times when you can determine what characters are thinking from their words and actions? Describe one of these times. Provide evidence from the text to support your thinking.

___

STRATEGIC THINKING

Reflective Reading
After reading this text, has your thinking changed in some way? Did you learn a lesson, change your point of view, or think about an issue from a different perspective? Explain how your thinking changed and what part of the text influenced you.

___

STRATEGIC THINKING

Changing Point of View
If you could hear this text from another point of view, whose perspective would you like to hear? Why?

___

Responding to Texts Task Cards

STRATEGIC THINKING

Fairness
Do you think the main character was treated fairly? Why or why not? Give examples from the text to support your thinking.

STRATEGIC THINKING

Judging Actions
Do you agree with the decisions made by the main character? Would you have acted differently? Explain your thinking.

STRATEGIC THINKING

Important Issues
What issues do you think are important to the author? How does he/she share this with you? Do you agree that these issues are important? Justify your thinking.

STRATEGIC THINKING

Convincing Argument
What are three ideas that the author has convinced you are important? What evidence from the text helped to persuade you?

Create Your Own Responding to Texts Tasks

Morphology/Vocabulary Prompts
- How does word structure link words? Find three words that have at least one affix in common and explain how the word meanings are similar/different.
- Find as many words as you can that use the prefix **dis-**.
- Choose three words that were really interesting, important, or new to you. Identify their base/root and explain what it means.
- Find three words that are new or interesting. Use a dictionary to find the definition, a synonym, and an antonym.
- How many words can you find to use instead of the word "said"?
- Create a picture dictionary for your text.
- Make a chart showing different nouns, verbs, adjectives, and adverbs you discover while reading.

Strategic Thinking Prompts
- What are some things you learned by reading the text that you did not know before?
- What was the most important event in the story? Find three things that caused this event.
- What is a really important question that you had while reading? Did you find the answer? If not, how can you find it?
- Does this text remind you of a current world event? Explain, using specific examples from the text and events from the world.
- Does this text remind you of another text you have read? What are the similarities and differences between the texts?
- Describe a time when you felt like a person in the text. Use details from the text and your own ideas to explain your thinking.
- What character trait do you think was the most important for the main character to have? Use examples from the text to explain how he/she showed this trait.
- Does the main character change from the beginning of the book to the end? How do they change? Use examples from the book and your own ideas to explain your thinking.
- What do you think is the main idea or lesson that can be learned from the text? Use evidence from the text and your own ideas to explain your thinking.
- Think about an important decision one of the characters had to make in the book. What factors influenced this decision? Do you agree with the decision the character made?
- If you were the author, what might you have changed in the book? Was there more information that you needed about a particular thing? Were there questions that you feel were left unanswered?
- Do you think the ending is fair to all the characters?
- What do you think motivated the author to write this text?
- Which character do you think was most important to the plot? Why?
- What are some of the traits you admire most about one of the characters in the story? If this was a real person, would you choose him/her as a friend? Why or why not?

7 Flexible Small-Group Instruction

As educators, we are good at helping students make progress, but not catch-up levels of progress. So the question becomes, how do we maximize our instructional time with students to provide a Multi-Tiered System of Supports (MTSS) and close gaps for our students as effectively as possible?

Small-group instruction is the vehicle through which teachers can monitor individual students and provide them with differentiated instruction based on their strengths and needs. By meeting with students regularly, we are able to determine which areas are their strengths and to pinpoint areas for further instruction or intervention. Small groups allow students time to share their learning with their peers and to give and receive feedback with each other. They can use this time to set individual learning goals and monitor their progress in achieving the goals they have previously set. From an assessment perspective, small groups give you a practical way to assess students regularly and use these observations to guide instruction, form new groups, and individually tailor instructions to better suit the needs of each learner.

Students can use the vehicle of talk to share their thoughts about texts. This provides the teacher with an opportunity to combine students' conversations and observations made during small-group instruction with the products students create during independent work time to form a complete portrait of each learner. This triangulation of assessment is important when assessing students' understanding and thinking, especially as it relates to comprehension and composition. Students are often assessed solely on their ability to read and write. Although the foundational skills of reading and writing are significant to students' continued academic success and their ability to thrive beyond the classroom, they should not be the only means of judging a student's thinking. Rather, teachers can use UDL as a powerful framework to enact the right to education and make curriculum more accessible for all learners. According to Novak and Rodriguez (2023):

> UDL is a framework for designing learning experiences, so students have options for how they learn, what materials they use, and how they demonstrate their learning. When implemented with a lens of equity in a multi-tiered system, the framework has the potential to eliminate opportunity gaps that exclude many learners, especially those who have been historically marginalized.... UDL creates a learning environment that is the least restrictive and most culturally responsive and trauma-informed for all students.

Small-group instruction often provides a safer place for students to engage in rich conversations about texts, their work, and their thinking. Through these dialogues, they are able to articulate their thinking, justify their ideas, even question and build on the ideas of their peers. This rich, accountable talk provides opportunities for students to expand their thinking about their comprehension and composition. In these focused, small-group settings, students are able to share their work with each other in a way that is nurturing and respectful. They are able to provide feedback to their peers, as well as receive feedback from their teacher. This instantaneous cycle of learning, sharing, and feedback has the most direct impact on student achievement.

Forming Instructional Groups

Initially, it is tempting to place students in learning groups based solely on their individual reading and writing abilities. In the past, this was probably the easiest and most practical way to group students since guided-reading resources were often designed to differentiate by reading level and provided a good starting point for grouping students.

However, given the research and evidence that we have shared throughout this book, it is clear that there are many ways to group students. By removing the teacher from the Purposeful Practice Time cycle, we are better able to be purposeful and flexible in the opportunities we provide for facilitating such strategies as targeted skill interventions, extensions of class learning, repeated practice, cross-curricular learning, pre-teaching or reteaching, and one-on-one conferences. Groups for Purposeful Practice Time can be built with students' abilities in mind while also making it easier to consider classroom management strategies and classroom dynamics since students will be pulled from various groups to meet with the teacher in a much more fluid and flexible manner.

What if students were grouped according to their personal interests? The teacher would be able to select texts for partner-reading times that reflect the specific interests of the students within the group. For example, some students become very excited at the idea of reading nonfiction information about snakes, whereas others are repulsed. Some students eagerly read fiction stories about magic, whereas their counterparts find this kind of text disturbing. If students' choices are reflected in the texts they are asked to engage with, no doubt their motivation and engagement will be heightened.

When grouping students, in many instances it is vital to analyze each students' current areas of strength and areas of need carefully. When reading, for example, some students struggle to decode words with vowel teams, some lack fluency and expression or ignore punctuation when they read aloud, whereas others decode beautifully but lack comprehension of the material they are responding to. By clustering students according to their specific instructional needs for small-group instruction, the teacher can spend time explicitly addressing these needs with each group of students. It is also helpful for students to engage in conversations with their peers, realizing that everyone is working on strengthening their skills but in different areas.

As groups are initiated, it is important to impress upon students that these are not "forever" groups. Once literacy routines are established, frequently revisit student groupings and regroup students as necessary. As students learn things and different skills become the instructional focus throughout the year, the way you group students should reflect the changing dynamics of the classroom. On average, Purposeful Practice Time student groupings should change monthly,

A Group by Any Other Name
Like it or not, labels are important. When forming groups, consider using creative group names rather than color names or numbers (for example, the Red group, or Group #1), which students might equate with ability levels or even rankings. If you use a set of names that follow a class theme or mimic the school team identity, students will take greater pride in their association with their group; for example, teams named after popular sports teams, mythical creatures, types of storms, animals, planets. Of course, ensure that all group names have a positive connotation and cannot be interpreted negatively; for instance, naming a group the Turtles implies that they are slow. As groups change, students can be involved in selecting new names for the groups, or group names might reflect a current classroom theme.

while small-group instructional clusters will likely change more frequently. Students make the most rapid development as learners through these short, focused, explicit teaching opportunities. As they develop the skill a group is focused on, it might not be necessary to continue to pull them for that targeted intervention. By regularly assessing their progress and re-evaluating their needs, you ensure that the time students spend in small-group instruction is most valuable.

Purposeful Practice Groupings

The purpose of these groups is not to "work with teacher." This is not to say that you can't work with these groupings of students. However, the teacher is intentionally removed from the cycle of Purposeful Practice Time in order to allow you, the educator, to be more flexible and responsive in the groupings of students who receive targeted, small-group instruction. You don't need to constantly change your tracking chart just because an instructional small group might shift.

During Purposeful Practice Time, the groupings we choose to place students in will take into account a number of different factors. If we want students who are struggling with fluency to benefit from the modelling of others, they need to have opportunities to work with those peers and share their thinking with students of different abilities. If we want to ensure our students are engaged, student grouping at times needs to reflect the interests of the students. Also, there may be times when students at different instructional levels are all working on similar individual learning goals and can be placed into groups according to these goals. Therefore, while we're working to maximize students' ability to apply their self-regulation strategies, groupings don't have to be homogenous in terms of their skill level. We need to allow and encourage students to work collaboratively with various students and not feel that the grouping reflects where they fit in the hierarchy of abilities in the classroom.

Small-Group Instructional Clusters

On the other hand, the purpose of these clusters (or groupings) is to provide targeted Tier 2 or Tier 3 instruction from MTSS in focused areas of learning. One-on-one instruction is certainly an ideal way to support the individual needs of students. However, with the limited time that we have, educators must consider the ways that we can group students with similar instructional needs in order to provide Tier 2 or Tier 3 levels of support with effectiveness and efficiency. When planning for this instruction, it will be important to consider your class portrait and the various areas of need within your class.

So, how will you determine your small-group clusters for instruction? To start, you may wish to create various homogeneous groups when focusing on targeted skills like decoding or morphology, so students clustered together are at a similar instructional point. Conversely, there are also benefits of heterogeneous clusters for areas such as vocabulary or fluency, where a mix of abilities in one group can enrich the learning experience. Remember that the goal is always to build your clusters with your instructional focus at the centre. You need to use your professional judgment to create dynamic arrangements that best support every student.

The flexibility of these small-group clusters is also significant. It is more than reasonable for clusters to change regularly because student needs are constantly changing. Since students are all in purposeful practice groupings working on various independent and collaborative tasks, it is much easier to "drop" a student from an instructional cluster since you won't need to rearrange your entire tracking board to allow for the change. Ongoing assessments for learning are the key to ensuring that we are supporting students with the right types and amounts of instruction. Whether you are using a formal process to monitor progress or collect various assessments for learning to inform your judgment, knowing the needs of your students helps teachers to plan effective small-group instruction. By strategically grouping students and regularly collecting assessment data through conversations, observations, and various products, you are able to maximize this instructional time and provide opportunities for students to learn from and with each other.

Small-Group Instruction and Intervention

Small-group instruction is a support provided in all three tiers of MTSS, becoming more frequent and intensive as teachers move from Tier 1 to Tier 2 to Tier 3 within the system. In Tier 1, small-group instruction can serve to extend the learning from whole-class lessons. These opportunities for instruction allow your students to deepen understanding, apply new knowledge, or explore concepts in greater detail, benefiting all learners by taking the learning further. In Tier 2, you might engage in small-group instruction with a group of students to offer additional instruction or practice related to whole-class learning. This is not about closing a gap, but rather to provide more opportunities to apply a concept or skill first introduced through whole-class instruction. Also in Tier 2 and into Tier 3, small-group intervention allows you to be responsive to students whose instructional needs differ from their peers. By using evidence-based assessments to pinpoint precise learning needs, teachers can deliver targeted intervention to close specific skill gaps and offer a more focused approach for a handful of students. Understanding these three purposes will help you strategically design your small-group instruction and use MTSS to meet the diverse needs of every learner in your classroom.

The goal of guided instruction is to equip students with skills and strategies they will transfer into their independent reading. It is a crucial link in the sequence of the gradual release of responsibility. Teachers can use this instructional time to monitor and support each student in their learning. Small-group instruction lessons should enable students to make explicit connections between the skills they are learning with the teacher and the ones that they are practicing on their own, and in turn to directly transfer that learning. This is also why flexible grouping is central to this model, with small-group clusters changing regularly to match learning goals and shifting student needs. Whether mixed ability or similar ability, groups are determined by ongoing assessments for learning, ensuring students receive tailored support. You will use various data, through observations, conversations, and products, to make professional judgments about effective group configurations.

A typical small-group instruction or intervention lesson can range anywhere from 7 to 15 minutes, depending on the purpose of the instruction or intervention. Although it is important to plan your lessons in advance, it is essential that the lessons also be flexible enough to allow you to modify as needed. When you observe students reading, engaging in conversations, or providing feedback to peers, you will be able to monitor the students' learning and adjust the instruction as needed. It is also important to remember that we can use a variety of

Possible foci for small-group instruction:
- Decoding/Encoding
- Fluency
- Background knowledge (facts, concepts, curriculum context, etc.)
- Vocabulary (whole word and morphology)
- Language structures (syntax, semantics, etc.)
- Literacy knowledge (print concepts, genres, etc.)
- Text structures (forms, patterns of organization, etc.)
- Critical thinking in writing (researching and summarizing text to inform a composition; generating and organizing ideas to compose)
- Writing craft (word choice, literary devices, etc.)
- Transcription (handwriting and keyboarding skills)

resources to support this small-group instruction, including texts related to other content areas, and repurposing levelled texts to support content instruction.

Teachers can also use small-group instruction for composition conferences that allow students time to share their work and provide feedback to each other. The teacher can use this time for focused instruction and individualized goal-setting for each student. As students share their compositions, the teacher can monitor each student's learning, provide immediate feedback, and assist the student in setting realistic goals for continued learning.

In terms of comprehension, small-group instruction is the time when teachers are able to interact personally with students about texts. Teacher and students can read together, think together, and share their ideas while interacting with the text. Teachers can monitor students' progress and use this ongoing assessment to inform their instruction.

When considering the foundations of language, a small-group instructional focus can be anything from decoding/encoding intervention, to identifying and applying structures of language, to building the critical thinking skills necessary for composition (researching, summarizing, organizing ideas, and so on). While many pre-made activities, prompts, and questions are available for teachers to use, they should always be considered a starting point. Teachers are encouraged to formulate lessons and activities that are personalized to each group of students and relate specifically to each skill and resource being considered and utilized.

8

Feedback and Assessment

There was a time when my students would ask, "Why didn't I get an A on this?" I often found myself scrambling to justify a grade and desperately trying to explain which elements might have been missing from the piece of work. Fortunately, that question seems to have disappeared from my students' minds, because they no longer need me to justify their marks. Instead, they are able to articulate their own learning goals, successes, and areas for continued improvement. When students become reflective learners, they are much more able to understand the requirements of various tasks and to articulate their learning in terms of these targets.

When they are taught to begin with the end in mind, students are able to develop a clear understanding of expectations and learning outcomes, as well as the ways in which they will demonstrate their learning. This allows them to understand how their work will be assessed and to perceive it as purposeful, valuable, and authentic. As young learners, they need to understand their learning target, identify the components that make the work successful, and receive feedback along the way.

Beginning with the End in Mind

When we involve students in setting the learning targets, they become active participants rather than passive observers in the assessment process. This allows for ongoing dialogue between students and teacher—there are no surprises when it comes to assessment. Students have a clear understanding of the target, and they can describe what they need to do to reach it. When you involve students in understanding the criteria for success and actively participating in creating the tools with which they will be evaluated, they can have a clear understanding of the skills they are learning, as well as the way in which they will be assessed.

Anne Davies (2020) believes that, in order to support learning, classroom assessment needs to involve students in the assessment process by providing specific descriptive feedback during the learning. Students need to know what they already know, what they need to learn, and what it will look like when they have learned it. Being involved in setting success criteria, they are able to use them to guide their own learning by setting personal learning goals, collecting evidence of their learning, and sharing their learning with others.

When we centre students' involvement in assessment *for* and *as* learning, they become self-reflective, self-monitoring learners who assume more responsibility for their learning. They show greater engagement and a deeper understanding

> "The primary purpose of assessment and evaluation is to improve student learning." (Ontario Ministry of Education, 2010, p. 6)

of their strengths and needs as learners. They are able to articulate their learning and use assessment as a tool from which they can continue to learn, rather than limiting the assessment process to a final summative evaluation. This allows them to point out the features in their work that they think are strong and to set goals for their continued growth. No longer do they ask, "Why didn't I get an A on this?" Instead, they explain for themselves the things they did well and the things they will continue to work on.

Learning Goals and Success Criteria

According to *Growing Success*, "student learning is assessed and evaluated according to the clear standards outlined in the curriculum expectations (the content standards) provided in all curriculum documents for Grades 1 to 12" (Ontario Ministry of Education, 2010, p. 7). Therefore, when creating learning goals and success criteria for students' independent tasks, teachers must be sure to use curriculum expectations explicitly to ensure we are assessing what we think we are assessing. Throughout the rest of this chapter, you will see examples of learning goals and success criteria in student-friendly language using the Ontario Language Curriculum (2023). Specifically, the ones following are communicated so you can see the application of the expectations to the learning goal and success criteria created. In each teacher's classroom, it will be vital to use their own curriculum documents to suitably apply this process.

Learning goals should be communicated in student-friendly language and come from the overall expectations that students are to achieve by the end of a period of time. For example, Ontario curriculum documents state that students should meet overall curriculum expectations by the end of the grade year. The expectations should also be accompanied by success criteria that help students and teachers be on the same page for assessment for learning. These criteria come from the specific curriculum expectations that can assist students and teachers in understanding the depth and breadth demonstrated in meeting the learning goal. This is also a crucial part of the gradual release of responsibility. Through the use of direct instruction, modelled samples, and co-created exemplars, students and teachers develop distinct expectations for learning and the communication of knowledge and understanding and how students will demonstrate the variety of skills outlined in the curriculum.

It is also important to maintain an asset-based lens when we determine what students can do in relation to expectations. It is sometimes hard to separate the strands of the rope and teachers often assess comprehension within a students' ability to decode a text. We must be sure to provide various text forms to allow students ample opportunities to demonstrate their knowledge and understanding in a way that works best for them. To ensure that all assessment and evaluation practices are fair and equitable, teachers must respond to the needs of their various students. If teachers treat all students the same and assess all their work in exactly the same way, those who require accommodation to be successful will be unfairly disadvantaged. "Teachers' professional judgements are at the heart of effective assessment, evaluation, and reporting of student achievement" (Ontario Ministry of Education, 2010, p. 8).

Following are examples of learning goals and success criteria created using the Ontario Language Curriculum (2023) (Grade 5). I have highlighted the text used in the expectations to construct the student-friendly language that would be shared at the beginning of a learning cycle with students.

> **Overall Curriculum Expectation:**
> *C2. Comprehension Strategies: apply comprehension strategies during, and after reading, listening to, and viewing a variety of texts, including digital and media texts, by creators with diverse identities, perspectives, and experiences, in order to understand and clarify the meaning of texts*
>
> **Learning Goal:**
>
> **We are learning to apply comprehension strategies during and after engaging with a variety of texts in order to understand and explain what we think a text is telling us.**

Developing Assessment *For*, *As*, and *Of* Writing

The whole-class instructional time in the literacy block allows for students and teachers to engage in rich dialogues about writing. The time students spend exploring different forms of writing provides a perfect chance for them to examine a variety of writing samples and share their observations. Conferencing through small-group instruction is the best way to offer feedback to individual students, while setting success criteria should be completed as a whole-class activity, so that everyone is on the same page when it comes to the learning goals for each form of writing.

Through the use of mentor texts, exemplars, or modelled writing, students can develop a clear understanding of the learning goals for their compositions. Students and teacher work together to construct a list of features that make the work successful: success criteria. Success criteria are the targets students set for their own composition that will ultimately serve as a tool to assess their work. They can include targets relating to the purpose of the composition, the ideas it contains, the way the content is communicated, and the form, tools, and techniques the students use to apply their knowledge, skills, or interests.

The sample success criteria shared later in this chapter for each purpose of composition contains numerous "I can" statements built from Ontario Language Curriculum (2023) expectations. It is not necessary, and probably too cumbersome, to include such a long list of criteria for students at the beginning of a composition task. Instead, teachers should consider co-creating success criteria with students throughout the process of composing to ensure your lessons and independent composition time can be focused on attainable goals. Success criteria are meant to be composed in a working document and should be adapted and added to over time as new skills are introduced, consolidated, and refined.

Teachers might find mentor texts, student exemplars, and teacher modelling to be valuable ways to bring learning targets into focus. Students can use them to deconstruct various composition pieces and establish the success criteria.

Mentor Texts

A mentor text is any piece of work that clearly demonstrates high levels of success in the skills we are striving to develop in our students, such as a picture book by a favorite author, a video posted on the Internet, a podcast from a person of interest to the students, or even a letter included in a textbook. A mentor text needs to include recognizable features and clear ideas. It should be at an appropriate level for students to read/watch/listen to and try to emulate, as well as being of a manageable length. It should be short, effective, and clear.

The mentor text can be shared with the students through Composition Time. You might choose to share the text with the class or allow students to engage with the text together in partner or learning groups. While they examine the mentor text, students should be encouraged to note the elements of the text that make it successful. They might consider the specific form of the piece, the style, the voice of the author, the content of the ideas presented, or any other specific features that relate to the focus for instruction:

- Which text form does it follow?
- What text features does the author use most effectively?
- How does the author develop ideas?
- How does the author use description and clear evidence to support their work?
- What is the author's main message?
- How does the author make their message clear?
- What connections does the author make through their composition?
- What research do you think the author did to compose this piece?
- What do you notice about the author's voice through the work?
- Which part of the composition stands out the most?
- How does the author organize the content?

As students explore the text and share their ideas through discussion, you can help draw their attention to specific features that are important for them to notice. Through the exploration of text and the rich dialogue they engage in, students begin to develop a familiarity with the text's purpose and form and are able to use their understanding of the mentor text as a guide for their own composition.

As a whole class, determine which features of the piece are the most important. Use these to form the basis of the success criteria. When students share ideas, ensure that the success criteria are relevant and accurate. Although the students might make numerous interesting observations about the mentor text, the success criteria should reflect the focus for instruction and be directly linked to specific curriculum expectations. As a teacher, you will guide the discussion so that students notice the elements that are important and can be used to support their composition. At all times, keep the learning goals in mind as you and your students co-construct success criteria that will directly support the curriculum expectations for each set of learners.

By participating in rich dialogues and a critical analysis of mentor texts, students are able to engage in more insightful thinking about the composition piece. Their conversations will enable them to examine the text on a deeper level. Students can use the success criteria during their own independent time as a way to monitor their own work. The success criteria can also serve as a basis for feedback and further goal-setting when students conference with you. By using Composition Time to construct success criteria, students develop a common understanding of the expectations of the writing task and can use these targets as they work independently or to provide feedback for each other.

Exemplars

Exemplars are samples of student work. They can be very powerful tools, helping students understand the difference between the levels of achievement in relation to the curriculum expectations. Many students enjoy Annotating samples of work from other students. It is best, however, to use samples that are not from the current group of students, to ensure an environment where students feel free to take risks and explore their own writing and composing with confidence.

If students are able to examine multiple strong samples, even in different forms, they might notice specific features from each piece that help to make it successful, or they could look for things that different successful pieces have in common. For example, they might notice that all the pieces have well-developed ideas that are connected to the topic; they could notice that one piece has exceptional voice, whereas another has creative ideas. Once students have had an opportunity to explore the various samples, they can share their observations through a whole-class discussion to establish the success criteria.

Asking guiding questions can help lead students' attention to specific important elements of the work. It is important that you keep the intended learning targets in mind and help to direct conversations in a way that will allow students to focus on the features that will be useful to them. For example, when exploring exemplars of a report, you might draw students' attention to key features by asking them to notice how the ideas have been organized; to identify which supporting evidence is most effective; to notice which voice the author uses; to explore how the introduction and the conclusion are connected. By scaffolding students' thinking while exploring exemplars, you can guide them toward the desired conclusions. This inductive model of instruction is highly effective, as students feel like they have discovered the keys to success themselves.

The students' observations can serve as the basis for developing the success criteria. As you record students' ideas, point out specific features of the piece and discuss the ways in which the author included them in their work. In this way, you guide the students to notice the important features that will become the focus for their own compositions, their feedback, and their assessment.

The following samples of learning goals and success criteria come from the Ontario Language Curriculum (2023) and are coded based on the strand they come from. For example, the code *D1* means the overall expectation comes from Strand *D* and *D1.4* means the fourth specific expectation under the first overall expectation from Strand *D*. Individual teachers should use their own curriculum documents in order to apply this process suitably to their own classroom practice.

SAMPLE SUCCESS CRITERIA FOR COMPOSING TO REFLECT

Learning Goal	I am learning to develop ideas and organize information when working on a reflection composition.	*D1*
Success Criteria	I can: ☐ Identify the topic and audience ☐ Use various strategies (such as conversing with a talk-partner or making a mind-map) to brainstorm and develop details to be reflective ☐ Consider my chosen form when I select and sequence content ☐ Include content and details in a logical order	*D1.1* *D1.2* *D1.4*
Learning Goal	I am learning to create a text that is reflective.	*D2*

Success Criteria	I can: ☐ Use word choice or a specific colour palette to establish a reflective voice in my text ☐ Use elements of style, such as rhetorical devices (e.g., repetition, emphasis) to express my thoughts and feelings about a topic ☐ Use a tone appropriate to the form I chose	D2.3
Learning Goal	I am learning to select appropriate media, techniques, and tools to publish and present a reflection composition.	D3
Success Criteria	I can: ☐ Create a final text, using selected techniques and tools, to communicate my reflection ☐ Conference with my teacher to explain my final text and the choices I made to share my reflection	D3.1 D3.2

Created as an example using the *Ontario Language Curriculum Expectations* (2023).

SAMPLE SUCCESS CRITERIA FOR COMPOSING TO ENTERTAIN

Learning Goal	I am learning to plan, develop, and organize ideas when working on a narrative composition for entertainment.	D1
Success Criteria	I can: ☐ Identify the topic and audience ☐ Use various strategies (such as conversing with a talk-partner or making a mind-map) to brainstorm and develop ideas for the plot ☐ Sequence content in a logical order to develop the setting, characters, and plot	D1.1 D1.2 D1.4
Learning Goal	I am learning to create a narrative text that is entertaining.	D2
Success Criteria	I can: ☐ Use word choice to establish voice in my text that sets the appropriate mood or tone for my narrative ☐ Use elements of style, such as figurative language and literary devices (e.g., imagery, foreshadowing, personification) to create meaning ☐ Make drafts that include revisions to the content or elements of style to improve clarity, and focus ☐ Seek feedback from my teacher and peers to support me in making revisions to my work	D2.1 D2.3 D2.5
Learning Goal	I am learning to select appropriate media, techniques, and tools to publish and present a narrative composition.	D3
Success Criteria	I can: ☐ Create a final text, using selected techniques and tools, to communicate my story ☐ Conference with my teacher to explain my final text and the choices I made to share my story	D3.1 D3.2

Created as an example using the *Ontario Language Curriculum Expectations* (2023).

SAMPLE SUCCESS CRITERIA FOR COMPOSING TO INFORM

Learning Goal	I am learning to gather information and organize ideas when working on an informative composition.	*D1*
Success Criteria	I can: ☐ Identify the topic and audience ☐ Use various strategies, such as brainstorming and researching, to gather information to share ☐ Determine the reliability of my sources ☐ Cite the sources where I found my information ☐ Sequence content in a logical order	*D1.1* *D1.3* *D1.4*
Learning Goal	I am learning to create an informational text.	*D2*
Success Criteria	I can: ☐ Use an appropriate tone and vocabulary to share information ☐ Make drafts that include revisions to the content or elements of style to improve clarity and focus ☐ Seek feedback from my teacher and peers to support me in making revisions to my work ☐ Edit draft texts to improve accuracy, checking for errors in spelling, punctuation, and grammar	*D2.3* *D2.5* *D2.6*
Learning Goal	I am learning to select appropriate media, techniques, and tools to publish and present an informational text.	*D3*
Success Criteria	I can: ☐ Create a final text, using selected techniques and tools, to communicate the information I gathered ☐ Conference with my teacher to explain my final text and the choices I made to share information	*D3.1* *D3.2*

Created as an example using the *Ontario Language Curriculum Expectations* (2023).

SAMPLE SUCCESS CRITERIA FOR COMPOSING TO PERSUADE

Learning Goal	I am learning to develop ideas, gather information, and organize content when working on a persuasive composition.	*D1*
Success Criteria	I can: ☐ Identify the topic and audience ☐ Use various strategies (such as conversing with a talk-partner or making a mind-map) to brainstorm and develop ideas ☐ Use multiple sources to research and gather information to share ☐ Determine the reliability of my sources ☐ Cite the sources where I found my information ☐ Sequence content in a logical order	*D1.1* *D1.2* *D1.3* *D1.4*

Learning Goal	I am learning to create a persuasive text.	D2
Success Criteria	I can: ☐ Use word choice to establish voice in my text that is convincing ☐ Use elements of style, such as rhetorical devices (e.g., repetition, emphasis) to be persuasive ☐ Identify the point of view of my text ☐ Identify the perspective and bias shared in my text ☐ Include counter-arguments to show I can identify different perspectives ☐ Make drafts that include revisions to the content or elements of style to improve clarity and focus ☐ Seek feedback from my teacher and peers to support me in making revisions to my work	D2.1 D2.3 D2.4 D2.5
Learning Goal	I am learning to select appropriate media, techniques, and tools to publish and present a persuasive text.	D3
Success Criteria	I can: ☐ Create a final text, using selected techniques and tools, to communicate the information I generated and gathered ☐ Conference with my teacher to explain my final text and the choices I made to convince others.	D3.1 D3.2

Created as an example using the *Ontario Language Curriculum Expectations* (2023).

Feedback, Feedback, Feedback

Assessment, planning, and instruction are intertwined and a cyclical process. As you introduce new skills, you are continuously monitoring student learning through observations, conversations, and reviewing the products students create to demonstrate their learning. This ongoing assessment helps you provide feedback and guide students in setting new goals.

Feedback is most helpful when it is descriptive and skill-based, rather than motivational. For example, feedback like "Great work!" or "This is amazing!" might encourage learners, but it doesn't give any guidance as to how they can improve their work. Imposing personal judgment on a student's learning with comments like "I'm proud of you" implies that a student should be motivated by external forces, such as pleasing the teacher or getting a good mark. Feedback is most effective when it encourages students to reflect on their previous goals and measure their work in relation to them. Feedback that is evaluative, like "This is Level 3 work," can give students some indication as to the level of their success, but it fails to help students determine areas for continued growth and development with their learning. Effective descriptive feedback should assist students in reflecting on their work, identifying their areas of strength, and setting learning goals for continued improvement.

"Feedback is about providing a path" (Johnson, 2020, p. 51). As teachers, we recognize the importance of using assessment as a tool to guide our instruction; however, students are an integral component of this assessment process and they need ongoing feedback about their progress. As Johnson (2020) states:

> It's not about walking the path for the student.... While we want to give them a clear explanation ... when we jump in and correct things for our students, we are the ones doing the work, not them. In these moments, we are forgetting that struggle is a necessary component of learning. If students don't have to figure out the answers for themselves, they won't remember very much because they haven't had to work for it. (p. 51)

For feedback to be the most effective part of assessment, it needs to assist students in determining where they are in relation to the success criteria and what their next step should be so they can work to get there.

As stated previously, teacher and students might find it helpful to refer to mentor texts as well as success criteria when it comes to assessing their work. In doing so, they can consider ways in which the success criteria are demonstrated in authentic situations. Effective feedback needs to contain information that students find useful and easy to apply. If students have previously engaged in determining success criteria, they can then measure their progress in relation to these learning targets. It is important for teachers to set clear learning targets and to display them prominently in the classroom so students are able to continually refer to them. Determining learning goals and success criteria should not be a one-and-done activity as part of a unit. By revisiting and revising them frequently, we ensure that they remain the fundamental focus for learning. When we provide feedback, we are providing students with an understanding of where they are in relation to the target. We can help them identify the success criteria they were able to demonstrate in their work and the next logical step they need to take to continue to work toward their goals.

According to Susan Brookhart (2007–2008), "Effective feedback describes the student's work, comments on the process the student used to do the work, and makes specific suggestions for what to do next." Based on this, the following suggestions might help you provide effective feedback to students:

- **Feedback needs to be timely**. We need to provide students with feedback about their learning while the student is still thinking about the learning.
- **Feedback needs to be purposeful.** Feedback provided to students needs to be skill-specific rather than task-specific. Provide students with feedback about the things they will continue to have the opportunity to practice.
- **Limit the amount of feedback.** Don't try to correct everything; instead, provide feedback about the most important, relevant, and useful areas.
- **Relate the feedback to the goal.** Describe students' learning in terms of the success criteria and assist them in setting goals that will move them closer to their target.
- **Feedback should be free of judgment.** Feedback should describe students' learning and assist them in setting targets, rather than having the purpose of assigning a mark or imposing personal judgment on the students' work or effort.
- **Feedback should be in relation to a continuum of learning.** Identify ways in which students' work has improved and assist them in setting one or two goals that are attainable for next time.
- **Feedback needs to demonstrate a tone of respect.** Use a tone that demonstrates your recognition that the students are in control of their writing and their learning.

- **Feedback should encourage reflection.** Try to pose questions that cause the students to become reflective of their work in relation to the success criteria.

A conference is not a time when a student hands their work over to the teacher to have it corrected. Teachers often believe that fixing a student's work benefits the student in some way. Some conference practices include lines of students waiting for the teacher to edit their writing so that they can then re-copy it as a final copy.

As a writer myself, I can tell you that the most effective learning that I have done through the writing process has been through receiving queries from my editor. When a true editor reads a manuscript or document, their role is not to fix the mistakes but to draw the author's attention to areas of confusion and areas that need improvement, by posing questions in a way that causes the author to revise and rework the piece. It is not until a text is complete that the editor will fix the mistakes in order to get it ready for publishing. At that time, the author is well-removed from the text and need only review the document one final time. It is the querying stage of the writing process that engages the author in the reflective process. This is the most powerful part of learning. This is what we need to capture and bring into our classrooms.

When we ask our students to reflect on their work by posing thoughtful questions, we enable them to be an active part of the process rather than a passive observer. When the teacher corrects a student's composition, the student is no longer in control of the work. The student has handed it over to someone else to fix and therefore is no longer responsible for the piece. All too often, teachers get frustrated with students because they seem to continually make the same mistakes and don't transfer the corrections from one writing piece to another. If a student is not an active part of the process when the corrections are made, especially when they are grammatical or related to the conventions of writing, they are not actively learning; therefore, it is not realistic to expect the student to transfer understanding to a new situation. The student must remain in control of their work and be responsible for rethinking and revising it as necessary. Descriptive feedback allows students to see their work from a critical standpoint and reflect on their learning. If they are encouraged to set goals for further learning, rather than focusing on fixing errors, they will be able to apply this learning to subsequent pieces of work.

Conferences should always focus on the learner and the learning rather than just the specific piece of work that a student has brought to the table (literally and figuratively). Teachers need to tailor feedback to meet each student's individual learning needs. A student's learning does not occur in isolated chunks; instead, each assignment continues to build the student's repertoire of skills. As students continue along this journey, we can use their previous work as a measure for their new learning. They should be encouraged to reflect on the learning that has already taken place to set the stage for continued growth.

Engaging in Assessment *As* Learning

Sitting at a conference table and listening to their peers share their work can be tedious for students. Some students find this process interesting, but in all likelihood they will consider this a time of waiting for their turn to share. For example, if a teacher meets with a group of five students for a conference, it might seem possible to listen attentively to only one student at a time. In that time, what are the other four students doing? Are they patiently waiting their turn? Are they asked to listen quietly to each student's writing? Or is it possible to include them in the discussion and feedback process? Is it possible to engage *all* of the students around the table? How can we teach students to provide effective descriptive feedback for each other and maximize the learning that takes place during conferences and small-group instruction?

Involving all students in rich conversations about each piece of work allows them to share in the role of expert. Students need to be able to share feedback with their peers in supportive, respectful ways. The "Feedback Prompts for Conferences" on page 138 might be helpful when you ask students to provide feedback to each other.

Another strategy you might find helpful when trying to engage all students during a conference is to assign each a specific role during their time together. For example, if students are learning how to compose persuasive pieces, each student could be assigned a specific element of the success criteria to listen for. The Main Idea Monitor could listen carefully to ensure that the creator has clearly stated the main idea; the Fact Finder could listen to determine whether or not the student has provided sufficient information to justify or prove their point of view; a Conclusion Captain could listen to make sure that the piece has a clearly stated conclusion; and the Editor could keep an eye out for appropriate use of conventions, tools, and techniques that fall under the creator's form of choice. These roles could rotate as students share their work. With this strategy, students all actively participate in the sharing and reflecting process. They are all responsible for listening actively and providing feedback to their peers. Now they are not only learning by sharing their own work and receiving feedback, they are also able to learn from their peers. They can observe how others are working toward the success criteria and how they are setting and monitoring personal goals, and they can actively provide thoughtful feedback by posing reflective questions or sharing observations with their peers. In this way, the conference becomes a valuable time of assessment *as* learning: sharing, reflecting, and learning for all participants.

Tracking Student Goals

In a classroom of students, it becomes a significant challenge for a teacher to track and monitor each student's individual learning goals. We need to develop strategies that allow us to easily record and revisit students' successes as well as to keep track of their learning goals. You might find it helpful to keep a clipboard handy and take a few moments after working with students to record observations about their learning, such as a significant strength the student demonstrated in comprehension, or the goal the student set with their writing.

But if we want our students to be active participants in the assessment and learning processes, we need to make sure they are able to reflect on the feedback provided in various small-group instructional opportunities. A simple but effective tracking strategy is for students to record their personal goals on the top of the work that they are doing so it is easy to find when a teacher or student would need to refer back to them. Another option might be to have sticky notes or a recording device that students can use to write their goals down (with a designated place to put them, of course!). If their goals are handy, the next time students sit to write, they will be able to focus their attention on meeting that goal. It becomes a simple way for students to share the goals they are working on with their peers, as well as to monitor their goals over time. Flipping through a student's goals, a teacher can clearly see which goals the student has been working on, how long the student has worked on specific goals, and how that student has applied these goals in their work. Students could even maintain a regular log of their goals and evidence of how they have progressed as readers and writers. This is a valuable tool for students to use when they reflect on their learning over time, as well as clear evidence for a teacher to share with families when they discuss a student's progress. With this simple tracking tool, teachers, students, and families can share in a student's learning and support the child as they set and work toward new goals.

Feedback Prompts for Conferences

- What was your goal? How did you work toward your goal?

- What did you want your audience to notice?

- I noticed …

- I was confused about …

- The part I connected to the most was …

- I was able to visualize the part where …

- The part that worked well was …

- Your writer's voice was strongest when …

- What did you do well that created the results you wanted?

- Did you consider …?

- You really showed your learning by …

- Is this something you're planning to continue working on?

- What was your focus for writing?

- After writing, which part were you the most proud of?

- What did you learn or try in this piece that you'll try again next time?

9
Building Literacy Connections and Applications

Ali huddles in a corner and thumbs through a nonfiction book filled with weird but true facts. His mind races as he pores over the information.

Wow, it's possible to use elephant dung to make electricity. How do they get the electricity out? How did they discover this?

If a major league baseball is used for an average of six pitches, I wonder what a typical nine-inning game costs in baseballs alone?

If some frogs freeze almost solid in the winter, what happens when they start to thaw out? Do they just come back to life? Does it happen all at once, or slowly?

As he continues to read, his mind is filled with questions—questions he will need to resolve; questions that have made him pause, wonder, and think. How can he begin to find the answers?

… and the doors to inquiry have opened.

Ali heads to the counter and picks up a laptop computer. Within minutes, he is searching for answers to his burning questions. He knows how to explore and examine the information he finds. He has been taught how to evaluate websites for accuracy and reliability. He thinks critically and analytically about the information he encounters. His learning has meaning, significance, and relevance. He is completely engaged and actively exploring through inquiry. With the tasks seamlessly integrated into his Comprehension Time, Ali has read a variety of texts, questioned, explored, thought, and responded. This is independence in action: using reading as a catalyst for inquiry; using inquiry as a basis for exploration.

Meanwhile, **Indigo** is putting the final touches on her letter to a popular snack-food provider. In Science, she has been exploring various packaging materials and their long-term effects on the environment. She has researched different options and is more than eager to share her opinions with the people who make the decisions. She is convinced that her information is important and that it will challenge the company's existing practices.

Indigo's letter is formal and filled with relevant information, collected from a variety of sources and organized in a way she feels will best convey her idea. During her independent-reading time, Indigo has chosen to use online sources and nonfiction books to help build her argument; she uses her Composition Time to craft a powerful letter based on her findings. Her reading and writing are connected in authentic ways that allow her to compose for a purpose and for a real audience.

Indigo eagerly shares with her friends, seeking input from people whose opinion she respects, values, and appreciates. She wants to ensure that she has stated her opinion clearly but not aggressively. She asks if her background information is accurate and concise enough to support her suggestions. She wonders if she should address information she has found that counters her argument or if she should just ignore it. These questions guide her thinking and help to shape her composition: questions that are important and relevant; questions that can be answered only through collaboration with a community of composers. This is collaboration in action: a community where composition takes shape through ongoing sharing and feedback.

Authentically Developing Literacy Skills

Technology in the classroom should not be considered an add-on. It should not be a separate component of the literacy program, standing in isolation from the other learning that is happening. It should support and expand students' learning and directly connect to the content and skills that are being taught during other instructional times.

The use of digital tools—computers, laptops, and tablets—along with the BYOD (Bring Your Own Device) movement have made it possible for our students to have access and connect to the world. We are able to remove our classroom boundaries and connect, collaborate, and create with others beyond our school, city, or even country. The portability and accessibility of digital tools is making it more and more viable (and probable) that teachers are integrating current real-time events into classroom experiences. Digital tools are not a new element in teaching; in reality, they are no longer even considered optional. We need to use these tools as a way to teach our students how to interpret material they find online and how to create and share content in responsible ways. We need to teach them responsible digital citizenship and how to be critically and digitally literate when they consider the information they encounter. We need to help them learn cyber-safety and teach them how to locate, evaluate, and analyze online information.

By integrating digital tools into our classrooms, we are working "to ensure that students build solid foundations in language and literacy, develop their analytical and critical thinking skills, and reflect on their learning" (Ontario Ministry of Education, 2023, The Strands in the Language Curriculum section, para. 2). By structuring and designing a literacy block that intentionally incorporates digital tools and skills, we allow our students to apply their reading, writing, speaking, and listening skills in authentic learning situations. These tools are valuable when we teach students to connect, communicate, create, collaborate, consolidate, and critically analyze. The integration of digital tools into the classroom helps students become more globally aware, more proactive, and more engaged.

At the end of the day, we are tasked with preparing our students for roles and jobs that we cannot even imagine, as many may not even exist yet. (When I was growing up, who would have ever considered that you could make a reasonable living as an influencer?!) Therefore, it is vital that we use a critically conscious lens—that is, be aware of how social systems shape the experiences and opportunities students have available to them—when we examine our teaching practices around literacy as it "is not just about an equal right to read—it is about an equal right to a future" (Ontario Human Rights Commission, 2024, Executive Summary section, para. 5).

Transferable Skills

Students can easily access content, so learning can no longer only be about the acquisition of content knowledge. Instead, we need to think of learning as a dynamic process in which we are teaching students not only so that they will *learn*, but more importantly so that they will *become learners*.

If metacognition is "thinking about our thinking," how would we describe our ability to learn how to learn? Learning means much more than being able to memorize content. It is more about the process of learning than the content of learning. But how do we begin to define this process of learning? It is certainly not a static process, but one that is always changing, an evolving process. If we think of learning as having motion, a momentum that allows students to transfer the skills they learn in school to authentic real-life situations, it is no longer about the potential that students have to gain and recall knowledge, but now about the power to apply their ability to learn in order to continue their learning. Students need access to a range of learning strategies and skills that allow them to be flexible when accessing, interpreting, and applying the information they need. When we consider the Ontario Language Curriculum (2023) as a guide, there are seven significant and transferable skills that students need to practice and refine, which enable them to develop the momentum to move through the dynamic process that is learning.

CRITICAL THINKING AND PROBLEM-SOLVING

As teachers, we understand that critical thinking and problem-solving are indispensable skills for navigating our complex global world. Central to this is carefully locating, processing, analyzing, and interpreting reliable information to address issues, which enables informed judgments and effective action. The process of critical thinking and problem-solving not only deepens learning through authentic, real-world experiences but also empowers students to work toward making positive impacts while fostering their growth as constructive and reflective citizens. Students who engage in this process learn to work through comprehensive inquiries, systematically solve real-life problems, and competently transfer their understanding by recognizing patterns and making connections across diverse contexts, disciplines, and interconnected systems.

INNOVATION, CREATIVITY, AND ENTREPRENEURSHIP

Innovation, creativity, and entrepreneurship are essential skills that enable students to transform ideas into action and address community needs through imaginative solutions. These skills include the ability to develop unique concepts, ideas, or products to tackle complex economic, social, and environmental problems. Cultivating this mindset requires the development of creative thinking, experimentation, and inquiry research skills, along with the encouragement of a student's willingness to explore new strategies and perspectives. Students need to be guided to formulate thoughtful questions, explore solutions, and demonstrate ingenuity as they work to make discoveries and build upon concepts.

SELF-DIRECTED LEARNING

In championing self-directed learning, teachers empower students to manage their own learning journeys. When teachers hold high expectations along with a deep belief that all students can learn, they can help students to develop motivation, self-regulation, perseverance, adaptability, and resilience. Skills and strategies such as goal-setting, planning, reflecting on progress, and monitoring their own learning enable students to work independently more effectively and to act on feedback to improve their work. Ultimately, this focus on metacognition prepares students to become lifelong learners and transfer their learning across their daily lives.

COLLABORATION

As the skill of collaboration is explicitly named and evaluated on students' report cards, we recognize it as a vital skill that includes the cognitive, interpersonal, and intrapersonal skills needed to work effectively with others. These skills deepen as students apply them, co-constructing knowledge and meaning in various settings. Students learn to participate in teams by building positive relationships, accepting various roles and an equitable share of work, and fostering trust. This involves responding positively to diverse ideas, values, and traditions, managing conflict in a constructive way, and building healthy peer relationships. Ultimately, students are working to develop the skills necessary to share information and resources and expertise to solve problems, make decisions, and achieve collective goals.

COMMUNICATION

It is hard to consider key transferable literacy skills developed across the curriculum without discussing communication. Communication is the essential process of receiving and expressing meaning across a number of contexts, audiences, and purposes. Receptive communication can be through forms such as reading, viewing, and listening, while examples of expressive forms are writing, speaking, and creating. As students get older, effective communication increasingly demands an understanding of local and global perspectives, as well as societal and cultural contexts. Students can learn to achieve this by asking effective questions, listening to all viewpoints and ensuring they are heard, voicing their own opinions, and advocating for the ideas, knowledge, and languages of various cultures and perspectives.

GLOBAL CITIZENSHIP AND SUSTAINABILITY

Now more than ever, due to a number of factors, students have access to information and intelligence from across the globe. They need to develop an understanding of diverse worldviews and consider political, environmental, social, and economic issues as they strive toward sustainable living in our interconnected world. As teachers, we must cultivate engaged citizenship, along with a deep appreciation for global diversity so our students can learn how to make responsible decisions and take actions that promote equity for all, now and in the future. Moreover, students must recognize discrimination, champion human rights and equity, appreciate Indigenous traditions and contributions, and engage in local, national, and global initiatives in order to contribute responsibly to society and foster a better, more sustainable future for everyone.

DIGITAL LITERACY

Lastly, to fully prepare students for the modern world, digital literacy must be developed to enable students to solve problems using technology in a safe, legal, and ethically responsible way. With the increasing presence of digitalization and big data, digital literacy also means cultivating strong data literacy skills and confidently working with new technologies. Every time we scan, type, record, or capture something, such as when we use social media or other digital tools, we create more and more data and digitize our lives. The increase in volume, velocity, and variety has led to huge amounts of digital information that can be collected and analyzed, often by potentially flawed AI. With the scale continuing to grow rapidly, students will constantly be bombarded by data and will need to be made conscious of it. As teachers, we must encourage the selection and use of appropriate digital tools for various tasks, while also demonstrating for our students how to manage their technology use for well-being. It is critical for students to learn to manage their digital footprint respectfully while recognizing both the responsibilities and opportunities within our interconnected global society.

Digital and Media Literacy Skills

In order for us to effectively engage with the ever-evolving digital tools that students seem to have at their fingertips, a key component of our instruction lies with developing digital citizenship. The other day, as I was driving my daughters to school, my oldest asked when she would be able to get her own cellphone. (For reference, both my kids are under 10, so the simple answer for me was, not any time soon!) This was followed by a question from her younger sister of how old I was when I got my first cellphone. This interaction got me thinking about just how much the cellphone I now own differs from my first, received as a present from my parents when I was in high school. Gone are the days when a phone was only for making phone calls or sending simple text messages. The plethora of apps and social media now available for download with a simple tap of a finger put children much further out into the world than even a few short decades ago.

My desire to develop digital citizenship skills for my daughters might be stronger due to my instinct as their mother to protect them, but online safety and well-being are vital to the healthy development of all children. It is important that students understand their rights and responsibilities when they interact online and are given explicit instruction in decision-making about digital media literacy (along with boundaries) in order to protect their well-being and privacy. Before educators integrate any new tool that involves students or student data, they should ask themselves a series of critical questions to ensure its appropriateness, effectiveness, and safety. Many boards have their own vetting process that helps protect students while they still work to optimize learning and maintain professional standards. Due to the large number of digital tools often available even on an already vetted list, however, teachers should thoughtfully consider the purpose, privacy, equitable access, and pedagogy behind the choices they are making. The following non-exhaustive list of questions can help you get started:

- What specific learning goals will this tool help us achieve? How does this tool align with curriculum, learning goals, and instructional strategies? Is it genuinely enhancing learning or just adding novelty?
- How will this tool differentiate or personalize learning for diverse student needs (e.g., support or challenge students)?

- Are there any accessibility features for students with diverse learning needs (e.g., screen readers, adjustable fonts, color contrasts)?
- What prior knowledge or skills do students need to effectively use this tool? How will I address any gaps?
- How will I introduce and model the use of this tool for students?
- Is this tool sustainable (e.g., considering cost, updates, or ongoing support)? Is there a simpler method or tool that would work just as well?
- What specific student data does this tool collect, store, and share?
- Do I need parental consent for students to use this tool, especially if it collects student data?
- Does the tool contain diverse and inclusive content that reflects our student population and avoids bias?

By addressing these questions, educators can make informed decisions that enhance learning while safeguarding student well-being and privacy.

WORKING WITH WHAT YOU'VE GOT

I'll take 30 devices to go, please!

It's what digital dreams are made of! While we would love to have unlimited access to technology in our classrooms, the reality is that we all face challenges when it comes to resources. You may have a patchy wireless connection (or none at all), or you may struggle with firewalls that restrict access to what you consider to be the most harmless sites. You may have a school lab that houses all the resources in one place, or perhaps you have a set of devices stored on a portable cart that always seems to be in demand. Whatever challenges you face, the solution comes with creativity and flexibility.

Integrating digital tools into a classroom is not as easy as introducing a new routine like independent reading or composition. It takes coordination and flexibility among teachers and students. There will be times when students are able to access more devices and other times when they are completely unavailable for use. However, as with everything in literacy (and in life), we need to consider students' use of and access to technology a part of a balancing act.

The framework in this book provides a way to regularly incorporate technology into students' literacy experiences for about 40 minutes a day with as few as five or six devices. During Purposeful Practice Time, a tech time block can be designated for exclusive access by a group of students. While it might seem more practical to encourage students to use the devices for only half of the time and then allow another group to access them, the reality is that it often takes students a few minutes to get set up, log in, and access their work. If they are allowed the entire block of time (Purposeful Practice Time), students are usually able to sink their teeth into a meaningful task and have enough time to make significant progress. With this model, students can have a designated tech time at least once a cycle, ensuring that they have sufficient time to make their experiences meaningful.

Comprehension and independent-reading time is another area of Purposeful Practice Time that teachers can use to incorporate digital tools. Using devices as a vehicle to access text for independent or collaborative work allows students to use their independent-reading time to interact with various text formats. It also allows students of differing reading abilities to access their choice of text with ease. Finally, students having headphones can help to ensure that various formats do not distract other students as they work independently during Purposeful Practice Time.

Both Comprehension Time and Composition Time also provide opportunities for teachers to use online text or digital tools to integrate digital and media literacy skills into students' daily learning experiences. With one computer and an LCD projector, teachers can access a wide range of texts and tools. They can use this time to model how to interpret and create different media texts while they introduce students to tasks to work on during Purposeful Practice Time.

Regardless of how technology is present in the literacy block, it should always be an integrated component, intentionally connected to the learning happening in other areas. Technology should not be busy-work or a way of entertaining students. The time they spend engaged with digital literacy tasks should be important and meaningful; it should allow them to extend and expand on their learning and not to escape their responsibilities. If we want students to be responsible with their use of technology, then it is our responsibility to provide them with learning tasks that are relevant and important. We need to constantly revisit the tasks, build on them throughout the year, and use technology to enrich students' learning. Technology can be an incredibly valuable resource when used effectively. However, if not monitored and maintained, it has the potential to turn into a time when students are engaged and busy but not necessarily learning. Explicitly addressing the expectations for responsible technology use in the classroom, as well as providing rich tasks for students, teachers will ensure that students' time is well invested in supporting and expanding on their learning. We need to actively support our students in becoming discerning, critical consumers through the comprehension skills they develop to understand and create meaning from media texts, as well as innovative, problem-solving constructors of digital compositions that clearly communicate their thoughts and ideas with authentic audiences.

Applications, Connections, and Contributions

Students are better equipped to develop and apply language and literacy knowledge and skills in their daily lives when we use a cross-curricular and integrated approach to literacy instruction. By engaging in culturally responsive and relevant pedagogy (CRRP), teachers are better able to meet the multitude of needs in their classrooms:

> Culturally responsive and relevant pedagogy (CRRP) reflects and affirms students' cultural and social identities, languages, and family structures. It involves careful acknowledgement, respect, and understanding of the similarities and differences among students, and between students and teachers, in order to respond effectively to student thinking and promote student learning. (Curriculum and Resources, 2024, para. 1)

Furthermore, the Literacy and Numeracy Secretariat (2013) points out that, as educators, our role is to teach all students while preparing them for a diverse world. As we continue to move toward equity and inclusivity in schools, we need to affirm the cultural capital students bring to the classroom. The development of cultural competence and the practice of teaching from an identity-affirming stance are deeply interconnected and foundational to creating an inclusive and effective learning environment, enabling us to better provide relevant and authentic learning for every student every day.

As students explore identity and belonging throughout various subjects and disciplines, they develop a deeper understanding of their own unique identities. By analyzing diverse texts from a multitude of individuals and communities, including First Nations, Métis, and Inuit perspectives, students also develop their understanding of various viewpoints, knowledges, and relationships. In a constantly changing global society, our students' ability to understand and explain how the learning across all subjects is interconnected will better prepare them for their daily lives. The following chart lists examples of what this looks like in classroom practice:

SAMPLE CROSS-CURRICULAR CONNECTIONS TO LANGUAGE

Mathematics	• Explore how mathematical concepts are used in different cultures (e.g., Indigenous mapping, patterns in traditional art, architectural designs from various civilizations). • Review and discuss infographics as a class. Use digital media tools and techniques to create an infographic about a topic of interest. • Use morphological knowledge to review and learn new mathematical vocabulary.
Social Studies, History, and Geography	• Explore diverse autobiographies, memoirs, or historical fiction to explore themes of identity and belonging within specific cultural or historical contexts (e.g., Indigenous experiences, immigrant narratives). • Research advertisements and media from various historical periods and examine the tools, techniques, and strategies used to persuade the audience. • Examine maps as visual representations of the evolution of a landscape and determine some ways that the maps show patterns and trends of human settlement.
Science/Technology, and STEM	• Investigate the contributions of diverse scientists and inventors throughout history, connecting their personal identities and cultural backgrounds to their scientific breakthroughs. • Research the impact of human activity on specific ecosystems, then write a persuasive report or create a public service announcement advocating for sustainable practices, using evidence from the scientific research to support the students' arguments. • Discuss the ethical implications of scientific advancements (e.g., environmental issues, artificial intelligence) and discuss how different worldviews approach these challenges.

The Arts (Dance, Drama, Music, and Visual Arts)	• Create art pieces, dramatic scenes, or musical compositions that express the students' thoughts and feelings as they explore various texts considering themes of belonging. • Research and create linked movements to communicate ideas from the students' own writing or media works. • Research historical events or cultural movements and then create visual art, music, or spoken word that expresses the students' understanding of the conflict or activism; for instance, protest art inspired by a social justice movement.
Health and Physical Education	• Discuss how different cultures approach health, well-being, and community wellness. • Explore the concept of healthy identity development and belonging in various social contexts, including discussions around mental health and inclusivity.

By planning for learning experiences that intentionally weave connections across various subjects and disciplines, teachers help students see the interconnectedness of knowledge, preparing them to navigate a constantly changing global society.

A Final Word

If you're anything like us, you might stop reading professional resources too soon. It seems that once we have a handle on how something is going to work in our classrooms, we are so anxious to try it out that we assume we have gleaned sufficient information to just jump in. While that might be your initial impulse and you are eager to start, there will come a time when establishing a routine is just not enough.

Once routines are established, they need to continue to grow and develop, and to respond to the interests and needs of the multiplicity of students that will be in our classroom at any given time. While routines are necessary for getting things started, the simple establishment of a routine is not sufficient to keep it going. All routines need maintenance. They need to be revisited, tweaked, and strengthened. They must reflect the needs and interests of the participants and include opportunities for them to express their choices.

As you have no doubt heard before, the only constant in education is change. This common observation reflects the necessity for teachers to be flexible in the ever-evolving field of education. We need to be able to adapt to new technologies (AI is here!), pedagogical approaches, and societal shifts, along with staying up to date with the continual scientific advancements that lead to better and more thorough evidence-based research that informs our practice.

It is our intention that this book be an introduction to the possibilities for your literacy block. Through the years, we have gathered countless ideas from a plethora of sources: teachers, friends, colleagues, books, professional development sessions, and various courses. Although we've done our best to track down the sources of the many inspirations, there might be instances where someone has been missed. If this is the case, we ask for your forgiveness. Teaching, as with many things, is about creating a collection of types of knowledge for success and then refining them into a way that works best for you. It is truly synthesis in action. We take the things we learn and find new and creative ways to bring them into our classes; somewhere in that mix, they become our own.

We are thankful for the opportunity to assemble a blueprint for the literacy block by developing the knowledge and practices collected along the way of our teaching and learning careers. Teachers are some of the most compassionate and determined people we know. However, our constant need to adapt, and being driven to do the best for our students, sometimes leaves us unsure of where to start. We hope that as you read this book, you take ownership over the structures and routines and develop this learning to be the most effective within your own context. For too long, we did what we *thought* served students in literacy instruction without critically examining our practices to be reflective and critical teachers, leaders, and learners. It is now time to be better, while still remembering to give yourself grace in this journey. Maya Angelou said it best when she reminded us to "do the best you can until you know better. Then when you know better, do better."

It is our desire that, by sharing our literacy journey, we are able to set educators on a path to examine their own practices critically and ensure they are grounded in the following principles: that every student can become an effective communicator, and, through the use of evidence-based approaches, educators can provide students with the opportunity to build the solid foundational knowledge and skills necessary to achieve their full potential.

Professional Resources

Allen, J. (2002). *On the same page: Shared reading beyond the primary grades.* Stenhouse.

Archibald, J. (2008). *Indigenous storywork: Educating the heart, mind, body, and spirit.* UBC Press.

Archibald, J. (n.d.). Indigenous Storywork. Retrieved from https://indigenousstorywork.com/

Boyd, M., & Markarian, W. (2015). Dialogic teaching and dialogic stance: Moving beyond interactional form. *Research in the Teaching of English, 49*(3), 272–296. https://doi.org/10.58680/rte201526870

Brookhart, S. M. (2007–2008, December/January). Feedback that fits. *Educational Leadership, 65*(4), 54–59.

Bus, A. G., Shang, Y., & Roskos, K. (2024). Building a stronger case for independent reading at school. *AERA Open, 10.* https://doi.org/10.1177/23328584241267843

Can Scarborough's Reading Rope Transform the Approach to Literacy Instruction? (n.d.). Really Great Reading. https://www.reallygreatreading.com/blog/scarboroughs-reading-rope?srsltid=AfmBOorUAeyUj0Jv6winJx_kfZbuolhxmxv73SExYAszRcznp17tcmn5

CAST. (2024). *Universal Design for Learning Guidelines version 3.0.* https://udlguidelines.cast.org

Center on Multi-Tiered System of Supports at the American Institutes for Research. (2025). *Essential components.* https://mtss4success.org/essential-components

Curriculum and Resources. (2024, November). *Culturally responsive and relevant assessment and evaluation.* Ontario Ministry of Education. Retrieved July 24, 2025, from https://www.dcp.edu.gov.on.ca/en/assessment-evaluation/crrp-ae

Davies, A. (2020). *Making classroom assessment work* (4th ed.). Connections Publishing.

Donohue, L. (2011). *The Write Voice.* Pembroke Publishers.

Farrell, L., Hunter, M., Davidson, M., & Osenga, T. (n.d.). *The simple view of reading.* Reading Rockets. https://www.readingrockets.org/topics/about-reading/articles/simple-view-reading

Gough, P. B., & Tunmer, W. E. (1986). Decoding, reading, and reading disability. *Remedial and Special Education, 7*(1), 6–10. https://doi.org/10.1177/074193258600700104

Graham, S. (2009–2010, Winter). Want to improve children's writing? Don't neglect their handwriting. *American Educator*, 20–27, 40. https://www.aft.org/sites/default/files/graham.pdf

Hiebert, E. H. (2024). Enhancing opportunities for decoding and knowledge building through beginning texts. *The Reading Teacher, 77*(6), 965–974. https://doi.org/10.1002/trtr.2303

Hochman, J. C., Wexler, N., & Maloney, K. (2025). *The writing revolution 2.0: A guide to advancing thinking through writing in all subjects and grades.* Jossey-Bass.

International Dyslexia Association. (2019). *Structured literacy: An introductory guide.*

International Dyslexia Association. (n.d.). *Structured literacy instruction: The basics.* Reading Rockets. https://www.readingrockets.org/topics/about-reading/articles/structured-literacy-instruction-basics

International Literacy Association. (2018). *The power and promise of read-alouds and independent reading.* (Literacy Leadership Brief).

Johnson, M. (2020). *Flash feedback: Responding to Student Writing Better and Faster—Without Burning Out.* Corwin.

Lane, K. S., Buckman, M. M., Iovino, E. A., & Lane, K. L. (2023). Incorporating choice: empowering teachers and families to support students in varied learning contexts. *Preventing School Failure: Alternative Education for Children and Youth, 67*(2), 106–114. https://doi.org/10.1080/1045988X.2023.2181304

McAuley, Sangeeta, ETFO Voice, 2018. *Culturally Relevant and Responsive Pedagogy in The Early Years: It's Never Too Early!* https://etfovoice.ca/feature/culturally-relevant-and-responsive-pedagogy-early-years-its-never-too-early

McCallum, D. (2020, November 11). Making read-alouds purposeful. *Canadian School Libraries Journal.* https://journal.canadianschoollibraries.ca/making-read-alouds-purposeful/

Moats, L. (2019, Summer). *Teaching spelling: An opportunity to unveil the logic of language.* International Dyslexia Association. https://onlit.org/wp-content/uploads/2023/08/Teaching-Spelling-An-Opportunity-to-Unveil-the-Logic-and-Language-Moats.pdf

Moss, B. (2016, February 18). *Making independent reading work.* Literacy Daily. http://www.literacyworldwide.org/blog/literacy-daily/2016/02/18/making-independent-reading-work

Ness, M. (2023). *Read alouds for all learners: A comprehensive plan for every subject, every day, grades PreK–8.* Solution Tree Press.

Novak, K., & Rodriguez, K. (2023). How UDL Creates an Equitable Environment for Students. *Edutopia* https://www.edutopia.org/article/universal-design-learning-promotes-equity/ (Excerpted with permission from the publisher, Wiley, from *In Support of Students: A Leader's Guide to Equitable MTSS* by Katie Novak, Ed.D. and Kristan Rodriguez, Ph.D. Copyright © 2023 by John Wiley & Sons, Inc.)

Ontario Human Rights Commission. (2024). *Right to Read Report: Early Reading Screening.* https://www3.ohrc.on.ca/en/right-read-inquiry-report/9-early-screening#_ftn875

Ontario Ministry of Education. (2023). *The Ontario Curriculum*, Grades 1–8: Language. https://www.dcp.edu.gov.on.ca/en/curriculum/elementary-language.

Ontario Ministry of Education. (2023). Appendix A: Language foundations continuum for reading and writing, Grades 1–4, Overall Expectation B2. In *The Ontario curriculum, Grades 1–8: Language, 2023*. https://www.dcp.edu.gov.on.ca/en/curriculum/elementary-language/context/appendix-a

Ontario Ministry of Education. (2023). Appendix B: Language foundations continuum for oral communication, Grades 1–4, Overall Expectation A2. In *The Ontario curriculum, Grades 1–8: Language, 2023*. https://www.dcp.edu.gov.on.ca/en/curriculum/elementary-language/context/appendix-b

Ontario Ministry of Education. (2010). *Growing success: Assessment, evaluation, and reporting in Ontario schools*. Queen's Printer for Ontario. https://www.edu.gov.on.ca/eng/policyfunding/growsuccess.pdf

Pressley, M. (2000). *What should comprehension instruction be the instruction of?* In M. L. Kamil, P. B. Mosenthal, P. D. Pears

Sedita, J. (2019, December 1). *The strands that are woven into skilled writing*. Keys to Literacy. https://keystoliteracy.com/wp-content/uploads/2021/03/Article-The-Strands-That-Are-Woven-Into-Skilled-Writing.pdf

Sedita, J. (2022). *The writing rope: A framework for explicit writing instruction in all subjects*. Paul H. Brookes Publishing Company.

Seidenberg, M. (2017). *Language at the speed of sight: How we read, why so many can't, and what can be done about it*. Basic Books.

Smartt, S. M., & Glaser, D. R. (2024). *Next STEPS in literacy instruction: Connecting assessments to effective interventions*. Brookes Publishing.

Swartz, L. (2007). *Write to read: Ready-to-use classroom lessons that explore the ABCs of writing*. Pembroke Publishers.

The Literacy and Numeracy Secretariat. (2013, November). *Culturally responsive pedagogy* (Capacity Building Series Special Edition #35). Ontario Ministry of Education.

Twyman J. S. (2021). The Evidence is in the Design. *Perspectives on behavior science*, 44(2–3), 195–223. https://doi.org/10.1007/s40614-021-00309-8

Vaughn, S., Gersten, R., Dimino, J., Taylor, M. J., Newman-Gonchar, R., Krowka, S., Kieffer, M. J., McKeown, M., Reed, D., Sanchez, M., St. Martin, K., Wexler, J., Morgan, S., Yañez, A., & Jayanthi, M. (2022, March). *Providing reading interventions for students in Grades 4–9* (WWC 2022007). National Center for Education Evaluation and Regional Assistance (NCEE), Institute of Education Sciences, U.S. Department of Education. https://ies.ed.gov/ncee/wwc/Docs/PracticeGuide/WWC-practice-guide-reading-intervention-full-text.pdf

Willms, H., & Alberti, G. (2022). *This Is How We Teach Reading ... And It's Working!* Pembroke Publishers.

Index

accountability, 29–32
accountable talk, 94, 97
Artifact Box, 45–46
Ask 3 Before Me, 19
assessment
    assessment for learning, 78, 111
    developing, 128–133
    exemplars, 129–130
    feedback and, 133–137
    goal-oriented, 126–128
    independent practice, 75
    informing instruction, 90
    initial, 22, 107
    learning goals and success criteria, 127–128, 130–133
    literacy tasks, 30
    mentor texts, 128–129
    student involvement, 126–127
    teaching and, 70
    triangulating, 102, 121
audience, 44–45

background knowledge, 45, 69, 88, 96, 111, 112
Box of Inspiration, 72
brainstorming, 42, 47, 52

character development, 49
choice, 11, 12, 21–22, 47, 52, 114
classroom library, 103–104
collaboration, 94, 142
communication, 142
community-building activities, 16
Composing Prompt Cards
    Entertaining Ideas, 58–59
    HOT Topic, 63–66
    Inform Me!, 61
    Recall and Reflect, 55–56
Compose to Entertain: A Story, 57
Compose to Inform: Web Organizer, 60
Compose to Persuade: Logic Table, 62
Compose to Reflect: Recall and Reflect, 54
composition
    described, 14, 39–41
    entertainment, 49–50, 131
    independent, 68–69
    informative, 50–51, 132
    persuasion, 51–52, 132–133
    process, 39–41
    purpose and audience, 44–53
    reflection, 47–49, 130–131
    writing vs., 40
Composition Time
    audience, 44–45
    composition cycle, 69–70
    constructing, 70–76
    described, 15
    digital tools, 145
    direct instruction, 14, 41–44
    foundational language skills, 76–81
    independent composing, 68–69, 73–75
    instructional sequence, 70
    introducing, 17
    process, 39–41
    purpose, 44–53
    Purposeful Practice Time, 68–81
    skilled writing, 42–43
    stamina building, 71–76
    talk, 44
    teacher modelling, 41–42
    writing prompts, 45–52
comprehension
    described, 14
    digital tools, 144
    minimizing through talk, 95
    neuroscience of learning to read, 85–86
    outcome, 84–85
    Reading Rope, 85–86
    Science of Reading, 85–86
    Simple View of Reading (SVR), 85

Comprehension Time
    comprehension cycle, 101–102
    critical literacy, 83
    described, 15
    differentiated instruction, 89–92
    digital tools, 145
    direct instruction, 14
    gradual release of responsibility, 91–92
    independent practice, 105
    independent reading, 100–102
    introducing, 17
    literacy block, 86–98
    media literacy, 92
    Partner Reading, 101
    Purposeful Practice Time, 100–114
    read-alouds, 88–92
    responding to texts, 107–111
    sharing ideas, 109
    stamina building, 103–107
    talking about texts, 93–98
    technology / Tech Time, 112–113
    text, 92–93
    tracking board, 110
Create Your Own Responding to Texts Tasks, 120
creativity, 45, 47, 53, 141
critical literacy, 50, 93, 112
critical thinking, 17, 42, 51, 112, 125, 141
cross-curricular connections / learning, 52–53, 112–113
Culturally Relevant and Responsive Pedagogy (CRRP), 16, 21, 145

decoding (word recognition), 15, 77, 78, 85
differentiated instruction, 89–92
digital tools / literacy, 97–98, 112–113, 140, 143–145
direct instruction
    adding literacy routine elements, 30
    blocks of time, 14
    Composition Time, 39, 41–44
    Comprehension Time, 15, 90
    framework, 16–32
    importance of, 17–18
    independent learning, 20–21
    independent reading, 103
    introducing, 18
    mentor texts, 40
    purpose, 14
    Purposeful Practice Time, 24, 25–27, 102
    read-alouds, 88
    small-group, 22–24
    think-alouds, 95–96
    times, 16

emotional cues, 49
encoding, 77, 78
entertainment, 49–50, 131
entrepreneurship, 141
exemplars, 129–130
explicit instruction, 17

feedback
    assessment as learning, 135–136
    conferences, 135–136
    described, 133–134
    effectiveness, 134–135
    student involvement, 135
    success criteria, 134
    tracking student goals, 136–137
Feedback Prompts for Conferences, 138
flexibility, 15, 16, 21, 23, 92, 111, 121–125
foundational language skills
    described, 76
    transcription, 81
    transition activities, 77–81
    word skills cycle, 77–81

global citizenship, 142
gradual release of responsibility, 14, 25, 89, 91–92, 102, 110, 124, 127
graphemes, 77

handwriting, 81
higher-order thinking (HOT) topics, 52–53, 93

I Do, We Do, You Do model, 91–92
independent learning
    Composition Time, 73–76
    described, 18–20
    independent reading vs., 20
    introducing, 20–21
    routines, 19
independent reading
    assessment, 107
    Comprehension Time, 92, 100–102, 106
    digital tools, 144
    independent work time vs., 20
    keys to success, 107
    reading program and, 103
    small groups, 91, 107
    tracking Purposeful Practice Time, 27–30
    word skills, 81
Indigenous Storywork, 89
informative composition, 50–51, 132
innovation, 141

interactive bulletin board, 111

language comprehension, 85, 90
language structure, 88
literacy blocks
    building, 12, 18
    choice, 21–22
    chunking, 6
    complete, 32–33
    comprehension, 86–98
    direct instruction, 18
    independent learning, 20–21
    literacy framework, 13–15, 16–32
    100-minute, 10, 11
    Purposeful Practice Time, 25–27
    sample timeline for introducing elements, 34–35
    small-group instruction, 23–24
literacy framework
    accountability, 29–32
    approach to, 13–15
    basics, 14–15
    blocks of time, 14
    choice, 21–22
    Composition Time, 14, 15, 17
    Comprehension Time, 14, 15, 17
    described, 16–17
    direct instruction, 17–18
    flexibility, 15
    independent learning, 18–21
    Purposeful Practice Time, 15, 24–29
    stamina building, 18–20
    Transition Activities, 14, 33
literacy knowledge, 89
literacy learning / instruction
    comprehensive, 5–6
    elements, 5
literacy skills
    collaboration, 142
    communication, 142
    critical thinking and problem-solving, 41
    cross-curricular connections to language, 146–147
    culturally responsive and relevant pedagogy (CRRP), 145
    digital literacy, 143–145
    digital tools, 140, 144–145
    developing, 140–147
    global citizenship and sustainability, 142
    innovation, creativity, and entrepreneurship, 141
    media literacy skills, 143–145
    self-directed learning, 142
    teaching practices, 140–141
    transferable skills, 141–143
media literacy / awareness, 92, 98, 143–145
mentor texts, 128–129
metacognition, 141
morphemes, 77
morphology, 77, 78
multimodal texts, 92
Multi-Tiered Systems of Support (MTSS), 11–12, 101, 121, 123, 124

narrative, 59

oral language, 40
orthographic mapping, 77

Partner Reading, 101
perspective, 49
persuasion, 51–52, 132–133
phonemes, 77
phonology, 77
printing, 81
privacy, 48–49
problem-solving, 141
purpose, 44–45
Purposeful Practice Time
    Composition Time, 68–81
    Comprehension Time, 100–114
    constructing, 24–25, 102–103
    described, 15
    direct instruction, 14
    groups, 122–124
    introducing, 25–27
    putting it together, 113–114
    sample, 102
    technology activities, 93, 112–113, 144
    text forms, 92
    tracking, 27–29
    word skills, 79

questioning, 96
Questions Board, 19

read-alouds / reading aloud, 87, 88–92, 96
Reading Rope, 42, 85, 86, 88
reflection, 47–49, 130–131
Resource Station, 19
Responding to Texts Task Cards, 115–119
Routine Cards
    sample, 28–29, 30–32
    template, 37

routines, 12, 19

Science of Reading, 11, 15, 42, 77, 85–86
screener / screening measure, 22
self-directed learning, 142
sensory statements, 49
sight recognition, 89
Simple View of Reading (SVR), 85
skilled writing, 42–43
small-group instruction
    described, 22–23
    flexible, 121–125
    foci, 125
    forming instructional groups, 122–124
    group chats, 95
    independent reading, 107
    instructional clusters, 123–124
    instructional groupings, 23
    intervention, 124–125
    introducing, 23–24
    naming groups, 122
    purposeful practice groupings, 123
    read-alouds, 90–91
stamina building
    composition routine, 71–76
    comprehension routine, 103–107
    direct instruction, 18–20
Storywork, 49, 87, 89
Structured Literacy
    defined, 5, 11
    described, 11–13
    literacy schedule, 101
structured talk, 95
struggling readers, 86
style, 49
sustainability, 142
syntax, 42–43, 77

talk / talking
    accountable talk, 94, 97
    Composition Time, 44
    digital tools, 97–98
    literacy skill development, 94
    minimizing comprehension through, 95
    power of, 44
    talk-centred classroom, 94–95
    talk-partners, 95, 97
    talk-to-learn, 94
    texts, 93–98
    think-alouds, 95–96
teacher modelling, 41–42

Tech Time, 112–113, 144
text / texts
    analyzing, 92
    categorizing, 92–93
    defining, 92
    introducing and summarizing, 96–97
    multimodal, 92
    responding to, 107–111
    structure, 43
    talking about, 93–98
think-alouds, 95–96
Think-Pair-Share, 95–96
tracking board
    Composition Purposeful Practice, 76, 81
    Comprehension Purposeful Practice, 110
    described, 27
    sample, 28–29, 30–32, 113–114
    template, 36
transcription, 43, 81
Transition Activities (Bell Work)
    described, 14
    scheduling, 33
    word skills cycle, 77–81

Universal Design for Learning (UDL), 21, 103, 121
universal screening, 86

verbal reasoning, 88–89
Visual Schedule, 19
Visual Timer, 19
vocabulary, 77, 88, 96
voice-building strategies, 49

Waiting Room, 19
word processing, 81
word skills cycle, 77–81
Word Skills Task Cards, 82
wordsmithing, 49
writing
    composition vs., 40
    craft, 43
    skilled, 42–43
writing prompts
    cross-curricular connections, 52–53
    described, 45–47
    entertainment, 49–50
    HOT topics, 52–53
    informative, 50–51
    persuasion, 51–52
    reflection, 47–49
Writing Rope, 42–43